Katie! Good
you!
Thank
luck.
Sunny Jankson

"Susan Ashbrook was a visionary in the connection between celebrities and fashion. She created the genre with Film Fashion, when nothing like it existed. It was her brilliant concept: pairing fashion companies with bold-faced names for cross-promotion. Since those early days, Ashbrook has built her company into a world-famous operation, and has been copied by many, many other people and companies, in a practice that has since become a way of life in the Hollywood/fashion interaction."

—Carol Leggett, owner, Carol Leggett Public Relations

"Susan Ashbrook didn't just 'do it'—she started it! 'It' being the lucrative juggernaut of celebrity product placement. Conducting business with the ease of the friendly girl next door and the grace of the smart lady who lunches, Ashbrook singlehandedly changed the face of how to gain access to the plush and privileged personas and the lucrative exposure such access can bring. Ashbrook's unique insider insight and behind-the-scenes case studies of how she did it make for an exciting, eye-opening read."

—Linda Arroz, Makeover Media

"Susan Ashbrook has been a great friend and asset to the students in the FIDM Film & TV Costume Design program. She is able to share her knowledge of the worlds of fashion, entertainment, and film with the students in an organized and eloquent manner, and her generosity of spirit is refreshing. She always gives students an interesting and informative look into dressing the stars, whether as themselves for the red carpet or as a character in a movie."

—Mary Kay Stolz, creative director of the Film & TV Costume Design program at FIDM (Fashion Institute of Design & Merchandising)

"Susan Ashbrook invented the concept of celebrity dressing and was the first to take it to the luxury fashion brands as a marketing opportunity. The creation of her firm, Film Fashion, set the standard of what a celebrity expected when it came time to get that press-worthy gown for the red carpet. Susan knows where the bodies are buried—literally—from the insecurities of the stars to the heights designers will go to dress them. I had the pleasure of working with her when celebrity dressing was an art form and not about how much a star was paid. Susan's finesse and gracious style made the stars trust her, and she took wonderful care of them—making them as beautiful and sexy as possible."

—Amy Rosi, owner and president, Aros Communications

"Susan is an amazing innovator, connector, and visionary. I have been blessed to work with Susan under both the Moo Roo and Mary Norton brands. Susan and her team had us in the hands and on the feet of every A-list celebrity you can imagine. I have the most profound respect for Susan, not only as a professional but as a human being."

—Mary Norton, renowned accessory designer and founder of Moo Roo

"I was so fortunate to be introduced to Susan Ashbrook and Film Fashion early in my career. Susan helped me 'have the look' on my early red carpet appearances, and she continued to help guide me through Academy Award season the year I was nominated. I have two favorite memories: the stunning white Hervé Leroux I wore to the Screen Actors Guild Awards, and the funniest moment, when Susan and I both wore the same chic black Kenneth Cole cocktail dress to a party for the opening of Mary Norton's boutique on Melrose Avenue. Susan knows about style, and I am proud she is my friend."

—Taraji P. Henson, Academy Award–nominated actress,
The Curious Case of Benjamin Button

"Susan has the perfect DNA to manage the most difficult personalities and businesses in entertainment and fashion. Standing at that intersection, she built the bridge to perfectly merge the needs and dreams of both the brand and the talent, always balancing the formula to ensure a winning outcome for both parties. Her ability to understand ever-changing fashion trends and match that ability to high-profile celebrities made her a knowledge broker to many important celebrity stylists and couture brands. Her warm personality and accommodating approach made her a trusted source to many who relied on her advice for the most important fashion events of their careers."

—Tom Tardio, CEO and president, Rogers & Cowan

"Susan Ashbrook is one of the pioneers and innovators in promoting the marriage of fashion and entertainment in Hollywood. She has a unique and intelligent understanding of the relationship between art, commerce, and the red carpet, helping to catapult designers onto the world stage of the entertainment industry."

—Arianne Phillips, Oscar-nominated costume designer

WILL
WORK
for
SHOES

THE BUSINESS BEHIND
RED CARPET PRODUCT PLACEMENT

SUSAN J. ASHBROOK

GREENLEAF
BOOK GROUP PRESS

Published by Greenleaf Book Group Press
Austin, Texas
www.gbgpress.com

Distributed by Greenleaf Book Group LLC

For ordering information or special discounts for bulk purchases, please contact Greenleaf Book Group LLC at PO Box 91869, Austin, TX 78709, 512.891.6100.

Design and composition by Greenleaf Book Group LLC and Bumpy Design
Cover design by Greenleaf Book Group LLC

Publisher's Cataloging-In-Publication Data
(Prepared by The Donohue Group, Inc.)
Ashbrook, Susan J.
 Will work for shoes: the business behind red carpet product placement / Susan J. Ashbrook. — 1st ed.
  p. : ill. (some col.), plates ; cm.
  ISBN: 978-1-60832-144-5
  1. Product placement in mass media. 2. Endorsements in advertising. 3. Celebrities—Influence. 4. Marketing channels. 5. Celebrities—Anecdotes. I. Title.
HF6146.P78 A85 2011
659.14   2011928215

Part of the Tree Neutral® program, which offsets the number of trees consumed in the production and printing of this book by taking proactive steps, such as planting trees in direct proportion to the number of trees used: www.treeneutral.com

TreeNeutral

Printed in the United States of America on acid-free paper

11 12 13 14 15 16   10 9 8 7 6 5 4 3 2 1

First Edition

To my parents for teaching me a good work ethic and to
keep my feet on the ground, even if my feet strode Hollywood's
Walk of Fame and wore glamorous shoes.

With love and gratitude to my husband, who encourages me to take
the "E ticket" ride to life and pushes me beyond my own dreams.

To Gil Friesen, who thought of the name "Film Fashion"—
and helped me discover branding—starting with myself.

To my "dream team" of editors, Bill Crawford and Aaron Hierholzer,
who took my manuscript and made it into a book.

I've had the honor of working with talented individuals and
true creative artists—what more could an entrepreneur want?

CONTENTS

INTRODUCTION

When Sharon Stone wore a Gap T-shirt to the 1996 Oscars, her unorthodox fashion decision caused widespread wonderment—and huge demand for a $25 T-shirt. In 1994, Elizabeth Hurley went from Hugh Grant's girlfriend to an "it girl" when she wore the Versace safety pin gown (altered within an inch of her life) to the premiere of *Four Weddings and a Funeral*, landing her—and Versace—in every fashion magazine and newspaper. Jennifer Lopez's infamous green Versace print gown (cut down to her navel) caught the attention of the world as she walked down MTV's red carpet.

As the founder of Film Fashion, a company that specialized in pairing fashion lines with top VIPs in order to build brand awareness, these successes proved to me that the red carpet is an endless opportunity to promote my clients.

When I came to New York from the suburbs of Chicago, I had big dreams of being discovered as an actress. Instead, I ended up finding a whole new world—the intoxicating world of fashion. After a short stint at a public relations agency that specialized in event planning, I was named director of public relations for Los Angeles designer Richard Tyler—the "it" designer of the moment.

When I came on board, Richard had really made a name for himself. He had been named the fashion designer for Anne Klein, which for a California designer was unheard of. The first year he began designing for Anne Klein, store orders rose 30 percent. He counted many celebrities as customers, including Rod Stewart, Julia Roberts, Janet Jackson, Oprah Winfrey, and Anjelica Huston. Richard was magic when he fitted actors in his clothing. It didn't matter what age, shape, or size they were; he made them feel confident about themselves and always found something good about their body. He taught me the value of great tailoring and design, and he taught me how important it is that clothing fits correctly on the body.

It was while I was working for Richard that I had an epiphany: Actors and models have agents, so if unknown fashion designers want to succeed in their rarified, highly competitive world, they also need agents. Based on my insight, I left Richard Tyler and reinvented myself as a designer's agent to Hollywood. Thus, my company, Film Fashion, was born in 1994.

Using my typical midwesterner's common sense in matters of business, I landed early clients like Ralph Lauren, Herve Leger, and Escada. Film Fashion quickly became a hot Hollywood matchmaking firm, and I became a pioneer for product placement on the red carpet by leveraging Hollywood associations into international media coverage for clients. I have worked with some of the most famous names in Hollywood and the music industry: Angelina Jolie, Jennifer Lopez, Sarah Jessica Parker, Beyoncé, Halle Berry, and Rihanna, to name a few. I started out by representing big luxury brands and later opened my doors to relatively unknown fashion companies. My sole vow was—and remains—to never take on a client I don't believe I can help. In 2008, I sold Film Fashion to public relations powerhouse Rogers & Cowan.

Today, effective product placement remains an essential marketing tool for anyone wishing to create or expand their business. It doesn't matter whether your product is high-end or low-end. The Gap, True Religion Brand Jeans, UGG boots, Jimmy Choo, and Versace are just a handful of brands that increasingly rely on product placement as traditional advertising platforms have splintered and collapsed. Designers such as Stella McCartney, Herve Leger, Zac Posen, Marc Jacobs, and Juicy Couture have become household names in recent years largely because of effective product placement. If you have a product you wish to promote, there is no reason not to take advantage of this celebrity power, regardless of the size of your organization or the nature of your product.

Having been one of the pioneers in the celebrity product-placement business, I have learned the ins and outs of working with the stars to gain brand exposure and build sales. I have seen products like Swarovski crystal-encrusted phones take off due to effective product placement, and I have seen other products fail, despite the best celebrity-marketing effort.

In this book, I will show you the best ways to get the most exposure for your products through product placement with celebrities. I believe this tactic is an essential marketing tool today, no matter what you're selling or what market you are trying to penetrate. Celebrity marketing can work for a tire store in St. Louis just as well as it can for Armani. The principles are the same; only the execution is different.

One of the biggest reasons you are considering celebrity marketing is to increase sales. Celebrities can build excitement for your product. My clients consistently tell me that when they are pitching their product to retailers, the first question the retailer asks is "What celebrities are using your product?" A British study conducted by Dr. Charlotte De Backer established that celebrities are seen as being of a "higher status or more successful others," which means that people are likely to "mimic their behavior pattern."

My stories will illustrate how learning the fine points of working with the stars and the media can put your brand on top, increasing sales by capitalizing on the sway that celebrities hold over the buying public. I will share what I've learned from my years in this specialized niche—one that I helped create. I hope you will enjoy this behind-the-scenes look at the world of fashion and entertainment, and that you will learn some valuable business lessons as well. Now, let's step out onto the red carpet and take a look at the world's most glamorous—and powerful—marketing icons.

CHAPTER 1

WHAT'S RED CARPET MARKETING ALL ABOUT?

The global publicity surrounding the Escada gown Kim Basinger wore to the 1998 Oscars was my first red carpet home run, as well as my first direct experience with the overnight brand exposure Hollywood can offer. The Academy Awards are the Super Bowl of fashion, and connecting Kim with that pistachio Escada gown marked a fantastic start to my career as the founder of Film Fashion. I'd spent the previous four years building my client list and learning the nuances of my field. That night, all the right elements fell into place, and I witnessed a dramatic, firsthand example of the impact of celebrity marketing.

My story starts when Kim was being photographed for *Vogue* and mentioned that she liked a floral Escada gown that I had arranged to be at the photo shoot. Kim and her stylist, Jessica Paster, asked Escada to whip up that floral confection in black for the Oscars. After Kim won a Screen Actors Guild Award and a Golden Globe for her role in *L.A. Confidential*, she began to consider the idea that she might actually win an Oscar. Suddenly, a somber black gown wouldn't do, so Kim and her stylist started suggesting ideas about the gown's design and color to Escada on a daily basis. Since Escada is based in Munich, the head designer, Brian Rennie, decided to send one of the company's finest seamstresses to Los Angeles to work with Kim and Jessica. Within days of the Academy Awards, I arranged for a sewing machine to be delivered to the Escada seamstress's hotel to help with putting the gown together and fitting it on Kim. Here's how Brian Rennie tells the story:

> I cannot describe the sigh of relief I felt when I saw Kim collect her Oscar wearing the gown we had designed for her! We had actually made six dresses for Kim over the space of a few days, as she or the stylist kept changing their mind as to what they actually wanted. The first dress we made got stuck in customs for a few days, and by the time it was found, we had already made two other dresses. In the end, we set up an impromptu atelier in the Beverly Wilshire Hotel, where we brought in extra seamstresses who stayed up all night making the dress she wore. It was a last-minute effort, and the dress was finished literally only minutes before she got in the car.

The photos of Kim in that gown are timeless, and they remain a great example of what can happen when you successfully market your wares in Hollywood. "The picture of Kim in the Escada dress still appears today in many publications, giving Escada incredible publicity," says Rennie.

Having one of its gowns at a photo shoot with Kim Basinger was a big break for Escada. How does this type of introduction between celebrity and designer happen? This is the key question I had to answer as I started my business, and it's the question anyone who wants to win through product placement has to answer.

Any star promoting his or her next film, TV series, or book will seek exposure through a variety of media avenues. Expert publicists and managers will coordinate the photo shoots, while stylists will beg and borrow glamorous merchandise the celebrity will wear. The bigger the star, the more garment racks stuffed with shoes, hats, T-shirts, dresses, gowns, jeans,

Kim Basinger in Escada after her 1998 Oscar win.

AP Photo/Mark J. Terrill

coats, and accessories to create as many looks as possible. (You didn't think they wore their own clothing, did you?)

Considering the deluge of media coverage we have today, it's not easy to create a unique look that catches the public's attention. The star will want to fill those racks with the newest, brightest, and hippest merchandise on the market, and that desire is your ticket to connect with the stylists, the publicists, the celebrities themselves, and sometimes the husband, wife, boyfriend, or girlfriend of the star. Popular celebrity stylists have become more difficult to connect with because, like celebrities, they are sought after by everyone from the high-end designer to the budding *Project Runway* contestant. Getting a product into the hands of a stylist so it will be seen at an event like, say, the Academy Awards might seem like a task only for the "big boys and girls" of fashion, but don't despair. Dipping your crystal-encrusted shoes in Hollywood is still possible thanks to a variety of more accessible personalities and events, including reality celebrities, red carpet events, charity events, movie premieres, film festivals, and even Cinderella balls. We'll talk more about the tiers of celebrities and events in chapters 2 and 3.

> *"Fashion is not only a necessity but also a form of entertainment."* —ISAAC MIZRAHI,
> FQ MAGAZINE, SUMMER 2007

BABY NEWS

Sometimes in order to get the right kind of publicity, you have to think outside the box in making connections between designer and celebrity or product and celebrity. As Film Fashion grew, I realized that special relationships appealing to niche markets could lend a powerful boost to both celebrities and the products they endorsed.

Right from the start, I wanted favorable word of mouth and good public relations for Film Fashion, so I was picky about the clients I represented. I hesitated when maternity brand A Pea in the Pod asked me to help it connect with pregnant celebrities. Women were still hiding their pregnancies, wearing their husband's shirts or other hideous clothing. Some celebrities even went as far as hiding from the public eye until they had their babies and could bounce back with rock-hard bodies. I knew I had a challenge on my hands.

A Pea in the Pod specialized in selling well-known designer clothing made to accommodate growing bellies. Anna Sui, 7 For All Mankind jeans, Diane von Furstenberg, and other top brands signed on to get in the store and in front of expecting celebrities, as well as regular moms. Once I took it on as a client, I'd wait until an official announcement of a celebrity pregnancy was made and then contact the star about A Pea in the Pod. In the beginning, my job was to educate celebrities about the brand. Many of their favorite designers were making clothing for their changing bodies, so they were interested. We would offer them gift certificates of varying amounts to shop in A Pea in the Pod stores. A big star might get a $5,000 gift certificate; other levels of celebrities would get $2,500 to $1,000.

It didn't take me long to get the ball rolling, and soon the media picked up on it, too. To complement my efforts, there were in-store events partnered with the Hot Moms Club and feature articles showing off Oscar-winner Marlee Matlin in designer maternity clothing. I may have been slow to consider A Pea in the Pod as a client, but I'm glad I took the company on. It helped that my client didn't expect overnight acknowledgment and was patient. It took consistent, persistent effort for me to get a handful of celebrities in the door, and then to get the press to follow up with stories. (We'll discuss persistence in chapter 4 and working with the media in chapter 5.)

Mona Liss, former head of PR for A Pea in the Pod, summed up the importance of the marketing we did:

Celebrity marketing for A Pea In The Pod was essential to the brand. As so many maternity customers are also celebrity watchers, we knew pregnant women would identify with some "hot" celebrity who was wearing a fashionable brand that was available to them as well. Once celebrities were showcased in magazines like *People* and *InStyle*, it was vogue to be pregnant and stylishly dressed.

SHARON STONE *and a* COW-MILKING DESIGNER

Sometimes it's not just the product; it's what the celebrity says about the product that matters. New, unique products that stand out will always find a celebrity interested in them. I know the importance of getting excited about a client and its product; if you're genuinely excited about the item, the celebrity is more likely to become excited, too, and gush to his or her friends and the media. I loved "breaking" new products I thought would catch on in Hollywood and collaborating with designers. In a way, I felt like a treasure hunter, and when I found the jewels, I couldn't wait to show them off. At the same time, I threw back any jewels that weren't the best or brightest. I educated my clients by reminding them that stars don't want to blend in—they want to stand out. If the celebrity likes it and talks about it, your celebrity-marketing story has begun!

Well aware of her star power, Sharon Stone decided to wear an unknown designer, Donna Baxter of Elsie Katz Couture, to the Emmy Awards. Stone told the press the designer hailed from Seattle and milked cows. Not only did the story get widespread media coverage, but even the milk industry got into the act: The Dairy Association immediately sent Stone a case of milk to thank her for helping to promote cows and milk.

Everyone loves a good underdog story, and suddenly everyone wanted to know about the small, unknown designer who landed one of Hollywood's biggest stars. Donna couldn't have picked a better muse; Sharon is confident

Photo by PR Photos

Sharon Stone at the Emmys, in the dress
that earned her a case of milk.

in her fashion choices and isn't afraid to try an unknown designer's dress for a big event. Sharon loved discovering Elsie Katz Couture and wore Donna's dresses and gowns to other red carpet events.

Donna Baxter and Elsie Katz Couture had set out to bring visibility to Donna's brand through celebrities; they managed to get one of the biggest style icons to wear their dress to one of the biggest events in Tinseltown, and to make a remark that caught the public's attention. Thanks to that effort, they saw a perfect example of the far-reaching exposure that can happen when celebrities get involved in red carpet marketing. Just imagine how much bigger the story could have been—for Elsie Katz, Sharon Stone, and the milk industry—had Facebook and Twitter been around!

> *"Celebrity exposure is now global, twelve months a year, and continuous."* – TOM JULIAN, FOUNDER OF
> THE TOM JULIAN GROUP, A BRAND CONSULTANCY,
> AND STYLE EXPERT FOR OSCAR.COM, THE
> OFFICIAL WEBSITE FOR THE ACADEMY AWARDS

GET WITH THE TIMES!

Not only have the products and the ways of presenting them changed since I started Film Fashion, but the media has changed as well. To get the greatest benefit from placing your product or service with a celebrity, you, too, will have to learn to change with the times. What works today will not necessarily work the day after tomorrow.

When I started Film Fashion, I targeted some of the biggest fashion brands, including Escada and Ralph Lauren. Why? Because I knew they had a marketing budget that would allow them to hire a start-up company like mine and help me get it off the ground. I focused on clothing because people were always interested in what the stars were wearing. I was breaking new ground with my idea and was fortunate to work with impressive people with marketing know-how: Amy Rosi, formerly with Escada, and Carol Brodie-Gelles, formerly at Harry Winston, were brilliant at getting the word out for these companies. Initially, I would focus solely on wrangling the celebrity while the in-house publicists and marketing departments managed the written word and massaged relationships with editors. Later, Film Fashion became "one-stop shopping." I contacted the celebrities, confirmed what they would be wearing, and built a media list to get the word out.

The Internet dramatically changed my world and the way I did business. My job description went from liaison to majordomo as I balanced and nurtured relationships with all the players involved in a celebrity's image. The demand to borrow clothing and any product visible enough to promote became a monster that I had helped create.

Let's take a closer look at this monster to see how the business of fashion placement really works.

CHAPTER 2

TIERS *of* CELEBRITIES

For designers, finding a celebrity who embodies their brand is of the utmost importance. It helps to deliver the designer's aesthetic to the world, as that celebrity ultimately becomes known for her work with a particular designer.

The world of celebrities is a hierarchical system, and to find the right representative for your product, it's a system you should be familiar with. All actors are familiar with the highs and lows of a career in the spotlight; stars must look good, find the right roles, and have committed, talented agents to get on the A-list and stay there. For many actors, it's up to the agent to either find that comeback role or settle for *Skating With the Stars*.

> *"Your twenties are about your body, your thirties are about finding the right roles, but your forties are all about your agent."* — *BLADE RUNNER* ACTRESS SEAN YOUNG

When my career as a fashion agent was beginning, I needed to attract big designer clients and connect them to big celebrity talent to prove my worth right out of the gate, so I went after A-list actors, who often get instant press. An A-list actor is an established celebrity who is consistently in the public eye and featured in press. But there are a plethora of individuals who are lower in the hierarchy who may still be worth working with as you promote a product. How do you wade through the different tiers of celebrities and figure out which ones can put your product on the fast-track to becoming a household name? Let's go through the tiers of celebrities before we answer that question.

> *"The celebrity who has probably had the most impact on my business is Eva Mendes. In the fashion community she is an A-lister, and she is always front-and-center at fashion events. She always gets tons of fashion press in both the long leads and the weeklies, and when she wore our one-shoulder tent dress, our sales exploded."* —FASHION DESIGNER JAY GODFREY

An A-list celebrity is usually a major film star, singer, or sometimes even a TV star. The celebrity's fame resonates throughout the world. Some top names include Angelina Jolie, Brad Pitt, Reese Witherspoon, Johnny Depp, George Clooney, Julia Roberts, Will Smith, Nicole Kidman, and Tom Cruise. Inside the film industry, "A-list" refers to a bankable star. However, outside the industry, the term has become subjective and can refer to any popular person admired for his or her social status. To many, Kim Kardashian is an A-list individual because she is consistently in the limelight. Still, some film industry insiders would not consider her an A-list star because she derives much of her fame simply by attending events. Nevertheless, as we shall see later on in this chapter, even reality stars who may not conform to the typical A-list mold should not be ignored when it comes to product placement.

> *"The young have to know that one day they may be less young, and . . . people may lose interest."*
> —FASHION DESIGNER KARL LAGERFELD,
> QUOTED IN *WOMEN'S WEAR DAILY*

Photo by PR Photos

Kim Kardashian, an A-lister in the world of reality TV.

The B-list actor is someone who is up and coming in film, TV, or the music business. These new faces are popular with the media but have not yet had the opportunity to firmly establish their own image or align themselves with specific companies. Most teen idols fit into this category because they are popular but haven't showed that their popularity will last.

The C-list actor can be a young, unproven star who hasn't gotten his or her big break, or a mature personality who the public might perceive as being out-of-date. The C-list also includes the familiar faces who host entertainment shows like *Entertainment Tonight* or *Extra*.

Calling anyone a D-list celebrity sounds pretty bad, but Kathy Griffin struck gold when she won an Emmy for her TV series *Kathy Griffin: My Life on the D-List*. The D-list is made up of very minor stars who don't have high recognition by the public. However, even a D-list star can have a certain amount of sway over particular segments of consumers.

This might seem like a simple classification system, but it's often difficult to place certain performers and personalities into one of these categories. I've been working in product placement and celebrity marketing a long time, and I still find celebrities who don't seem to fit neatly in the A/B/C/D system. Celebrities can also make rapid jumps up and down in the system—perhaps they had a hit movie or song, or perhaps they were entangled in a reputation-marring scandal.

To help me in the task of ranking a celebrity's star power and reach, I read a lot of entertainment and celebrity magazines and blogs. One of the more helpful websites in this type of research is IMDb.com, a popular site that makes it easy to read up on celebrities and all the projects they are working on or slated to work on in the future. (A paid version, IMDbPro .com, gives you even more access to in-development projects.) If you want to know celebrities, bookmark this website. If you are considering celebrity marketing, start by subscribing to magazines like *People* and *Us Weekly* to familiarize yourself with the hot names the magazines' readers want to know more about. These weeklies contain a plethora of news on the hottest people in show business.

No matter what level they are—A-list to D-list—celebrities can bring attention to your merchandise. Each month, my clients expected some kind of press or media impression connected with a star, so it was up to me to be creative and figure out how to make this happen. Sometimes a client expected to see an A-list actor wearing its product, and if this was a realistic possibility, I was off and running to make it happen. But in my field it's important to be realistic, so I also had the job of telling a client if I thought it was reaching for a star even an astronaut couldn't get to.

HOW I GOT SPEEDO
on an A-LISTER

You have to start somewhere, so it's important to stay open to working with any level of celebrity.

Speedo is well known for the sleek, state-of-the-art swimsuits worn by Michael Phelps and other Olympic swimmers. However, the swimwear the company made for normal beachgoers had gone unrecognized, so it enlisted my help. We went through the catalogue of styles and designs Speedo offered and I handpicked items I knew would appeal to Malibu Hollywood. What did I suggest? Slimming styles and colors, because I knew anyone in the public eye is insecure about their body. My next step for Speedo was to put together a target list of celebrities. I always suggest casting the net wide, and in this case we compiled a list of actors, from megawatt to minor, many of whom I knew were athletic. There were certainly A-list actors on my list, but I didn't limit myself to just that category.

With help from the Internet, I researched celebrities like Brad Pitt and Cindy Crawford who have homes on the beach. I kept building out the list with names of VIPs who had been photographed vacationing on a beach. I included young celebrity moms, and when I sent the moms their Speedo swimsuits, I included kids' swimsuits, too. With my list complete, I began to "seed" the product, a term used by people in my industry to describe the sending of product in the hope that it will turn up in photos. Speedo hit the jackpot when Matthew McConaughey learned to surf wearing a pair of Speedo board shorts I had sent him. Matthew's photo was seen in the weekly publications *People*, *In Touch*, and *Us Weekly*, each of which boast millions of readers a week. Later, Hayden Panettiere also appeared in public with a Speedo product.

Photo by Pacific Coast News

Matthew McConaughey in Speedo board shorts.

Did we get lucky? Absolutely! Matthew is definitely an A-list actor, and Hayden could well be on her way there. However, by following my methods, this can happen to you, too.

Here are the rules I followed:

- I did not single out only A-list actors. I started with a list of fifty celebrities that I thought might be a realistic match for Speedo.

- I made sure Speedo was prepared to gift these celebrities with an assortment of two or three swimsuits. We included other fun Speedo-brand items like a nylon bag and swim goggles. Whenever I "seeded" product with a celebrity, regardless of who he or she was, I would create fun packaging so it was like Christmas as they peeled away the layers of tissue to find the gift.

- I warned my client that we could send product and end up with no results—in other words, Speedo knew this was a wild card. If we got no one or only a C- or D-list star who wouldn't have much impact, we would have to edit our list and keep on sending product. (As we'll discuss in chapter 4, it's all about persistence!)

- Once the product was sent to each celebrity, I watched celebrity websites that show the stars being "normal folks" and came across Matthew's photo. Success!

Getting an A-list actor to publicly use, wear, or talk about your product is a tough challenge. They are surrounded by agents who want their 10 to 15 percent for endorsement deals, so naturally, it doesn't come easy.

J.LO'S DREAM GOWN

In the tough landscape of celebrity marketing, it's important to be open-minded about all opportunities. Today's up-and-comer can be tomorrow's superstar—which is exactly what happened with Jennifer Lopez. Today, Jennifer Lopez is an A-list actress, singer, and entrepreneur, but when I first met her, she was an up-and-coming actor working hard for a break. Jennifer was getting married for the first time, and her stylist, Phillip Bloch—the original "stylist to the stars," with whom I had cultivated a relationship—suggested my client Escada for the wedding gown.

Escada realized they needed to prove to Phillip and his client that they were up for the job and could make Jennifer's wedding gown her "dream gown." Escada's dress was a huge success, and Phillip asked the company to make three more celebrity wedding gowns, for Angela Bassett, Vivica A. Fox, and Lauren Holly.

"I had no clue who Jennifer Lopez was when the call came in. Many designers were not interested in her and would not make her wedding dress, but I trusted Susan in her choice and was honored to make the dress. The first thing I'm asked about in interviews is how was it designing J.Lo's wedding dress! Thanks to that success, I had three of my celebrity wedding dresses on one wedding TV special!" **— BRIAN RENNIE, FORMER CREATIVE DIRECTOR, ESCADA**

My research into Jennifer Lopez was what helped me understand that she was on her way to the A-list. I knew Jennifer Lopez had four films coming out the year I worked with her and Phillip Bloch. That, coupled with my intuition, helped me make the informed guess that this was someone whose career was about to take off, and who could really elevate my client's brand. I knew about Jennifer's upcoming projects from reading trade publications like *The Hollywood Reporter* and *Variety* to stay informed, but that might be taking it a bit far for an amateur; entertainment magazines are a great start. These publications will keep you up to speed on who is popular and help you identify rising stars you can approach about your product.

I've had many clients who were asked to work with an actress they didn't know or who wouldn't have been their number-one choice. It's limiting to only try to target A-list actors, and it's getting harder as many of those celebrities are looking for brand endorsement deals.

I suggest considering carefully what level of celebrity really can elevate your brand and reach your fashion-obsessed consumer.

Lara Flynn Boyle caused quite a commotion when she appeared at the Golden Globes in 2003 wearing a custom David Cardona ballerina tutu. Yes—you heard right! According to *Entertainment Weekly*, sometime boyfriend Jack Nicholson said, "Lara's tutu was startling. But she's a very colorful actress." Lara might not have been David Cardona's first choice, but the dress caught everyone's attention—regardless of whether the feedback was good or bad. As they say, **all publicity is good publicity**. David was a small fish in a sea of big-name fashion designers, so in this case, the visibility his name and dress garnered was worth the risk to him. This might not be the right strategy for everyone, but it worked for David.

"Sometimes negative publicity can be used to your advantage. Many 'bad girl' celebrities get you more publicity than the 'good girl' ones!" – BRIAN RENNIE, FORMER CREATIVE DIRECTOR, ESCADA

SATELLITE STARS:
SPOUSES, MODELS, *and* TV HOSTS

The people who are nominated or presenting at the big award shows always attend with a significant other. It's rare that spouses of stars and even top producers and directors garner the kind of exposure and press that the stars themselves do for their walk down the red carpet. However, every agent, manager, and publicist has called me at one time or another to see if any of my clients would dress (complimentarily, of course) the wife of their director/producer/studio head. This is not a worthwhile direction if you want to walk the path of celebrity marketing.

I first learned about Herve Leger and his "bandage dress" by seeing all the top models wearing it. Herve had successfully sought out models he knew and worked with to start a buzz about his name and dresses. He didn't have the connections to Hollywood stars that I had, so we agreed to start working together. Models are certainly A-list in the world of fashion, but for celebrity marketing, they teeter into the lower levels. Herve had successfully dressed quite a few of the most famous models, so he made my job easier. I would single out photographs of the beautiful models in his clothing when I approached celebrities.

TV journalists with *Entertainment Tonight*, *Access Hollywood*, *Extra*, and *The Insider* are considered C-list, but with daily shows reaching millions of viewers, I believe working with these presenters can help get your foot in the door. These shows often help promote a designer who dresses their hosts and offer contests for their viewers for non-fashion products. Full-time costume designers are always seeking product for the talent they dress, and these daily entertainment shows offer giveaways in which viewers can win cool gadgets, trips, and other interesting items to create buzz and free advertising—often in exchange for gifting the product.

MAKING TEQUILA FASHIONABLE

Sometimes the nature of the product dictates the level of celebrity you will be able to attract. I've made my name by placing fashion products in Hollywood, but I've had the opportunity to work with some mainstream products and exercise my marketing theories for other types of products, too. Partida Tequila owners asked me to work with them to introduce their brand to Hollywood influencers by producing a one-night event. The brand wanted to host a formal tasting party for VIP celebrities and press. Family spokeswoman Sophia Partida wanted the focus to be about the high-end tequila: "We're moving away from the whole 'Let's party and do a shot' image into a more sophisticated area, teaching people how to enjoy tequila like a fine wine."

Baseball great Reggie Jackson, young starlet Arielle Kebbel, and soap opera star Rebecca Budig enjoyed the evening, but I knew it would take more than just a few stars attending the event to create a buzz. Since celebrities get paid significant endorsement fees for aligning with alcohol brands, I knew it wouldn't be possible to get any A- or B-list celebrity to attend the event, which would look like a form of endorsement to their fans. Instead, I targeted one of the top TV shows, *Dancing with the Stars*, which was a haven for C-list celebrities.

The show had just hit the screens and was gathering momentum, boasting thirty million viewers. I capitalized on a popular idea to add some glamour to an event that would otherwise be just another event. I contacted Cheryl Burke and Louis van Amstel, two of the show's most popular professional dancers, and asked if they would consider demonstrating one of their choreographed dances for the crowd.

Without a budget, I could only barter the tequila to the two dancers, knowing most performers at the lower end of the celebrity spectrum need publicity for themselves, too, particularly with only one season of episodes under their belt. In this case, the two dancers confirmed, especially once we offered up a list of editors attending the event. Their dance was the hit of the evening.

This kind of event can be recycled and reinvented in a number of ways, from small town to big town bright lights.

THE NEW REALITY

Stars from reality TV shows have opened a whole new ball game of celebrity marketing. Some are human promotion machines, going out every night to some event. Keep in mind that they are not trained actors and are probably getting paid for each appearance. So, if you are asking a reality star to visit your restaurant while the photographers and paparazzi are waiting, it might cost you. If you are interested in having them wear a fashion item, they will probably be open to freebies.

If you're considering working with a reality star on a promotion, remember that such stars have a very short shelf life. It's always best to strike while they are hot rather than wait until their shows are canceled, and some people—including fashion journalist Merle Ginsberg—believe reality stars and other flash-in-the-pan celebs might do more harm than good to a brand. However, despite the short window of time most reality stars have, many people have found success in using them for marketing. A popular store in Beverly Hills has been rumored to barter product in exchange for the reality star of the moment to shop there—making sure the paparazzi is waiting outside the store to photograph the star. Popular restaurants and clubs in Las Vegas host parties for Audrina Patridge and Heidi Montag of *The Hills* and Playmate Holly Madison of *The Girls Next Door* to draw a young crowd. My educated guess is that the celebrity collects a fee, or the venue barters first-class hotel rooms, airfare, and complimentary passes to the reality star's guest list of friends, in exchange for the celeb acting as host of the evening.

*"I think it's very important for a brand to work
with the right celebrity. A B-, C-, or D-level celeb can
cheapen your product and its image. Low-level stars are
a dime a dozen, and the 'fast celebs'—the ones who will
be gone in two minutes (reality stars)—broadcast the
same about products."* —MERLE GINSBERG,
AUTHOR, FASHION JOURNALIST, EDITOR-IN-CHIEF
OF FASHIONRULES.COM, AND TV SHOW GUEST

THE TEEN CROWD

The newest group of teen stars is a big influence on the kids who follow them. Teen stars change frequently, with a whole new crop waiting for their shot. They come from the worlds of Disney and Nickelodeon—from music, TV shows, and movies. If your product appeals to the teen market, it's important to search out what stars the kids are following. Britney Spears, Mischa Barton, Paris Hilton, and Lindsay Lohan were top of the list once, but no longer, because teens tend to follow celebrities closer to their age.

Appealing to the Y and Z generations can be very lucrative. According to *Women's Wear Daily,* for the twelve months between April 2009 and May 2010, teenagers and young adults thirteen to twenty-four years old spent $50.81 billion on apparel. Fashion marketers made celebrity fashion labels almost as common as designer labels, quickly signing up the newest batch of teen stars, such as Kmart's Dream Out Loud line with Selena Gomez and Walmart's line with Miley Cyrus, cobranded with BCBG's Max Azria.

To find out who is making the mark in teen trendsetting, visit www.qscores.com. The Q score measures the appeal and likability of a performer among those who know the performer.

Sometimes former child and teen stars make a big enough impact to continue to set fashion trends. Ashley and Mary-Kate Olsen started their

All grown up—the Olsen twins, fashion designers.

own fashion line when they realized people had been watching them since they were nine months old. They arrived at this decision when they were on a press tour in Canada and looked out at a sea of young girls emulating their style. They saw oversize sweaters, big sunglasses, and designer handbags—and the lightbulb went off. The Olsen twins may have their own fashion brand, but they can't wear it 365 days of the year. Their fans still replicate the girls' distinct look, and knowing this should give you pause if you're making those oversize sweaters, big sunglasses, or designer handbags!

> *"Celebrity influence seems to be increasing because of the sheer exposure and 360-degree access the public has to these personalities and their styles."*
> — KIT NORMARK, SENIOR RESEARCH MANAGER
> AT TEENAGE RESEARCH UNLIMITED

NO MATTER WHO IT IS, KNOW WHO THEY ARE

Once again, I want to emphasize that it's important to do your homework when deciding what celebrities to target for your product. It's always good to know something about a celebrity you are reaching out to. For instance, if you design leather clothing, you wouldn't want to send anything off to Chrissie Hynde of the Pretenders. Chrissie has been an activist for PETA and a vegetarian since she was seventeen—and definitely doesn't wear leather. The Internet has certainly made it a lot easier to learn more about the likes and dislikes of a celebrity. Alicia Silverstone is another celebrity who doesn't wear leather, so I'd obviously never send her leather shoes or a handbag from Kenneth Cole.

When designer Georges Chakra sent sketches off to Helen Mirren to design something for the Oscars, he was promptly told she doesn't do sleeveless. I should have spent time studying what Dame Mirren had worn in the past, since I could have saved Georges valuable time by telling him she always wears sleeves. I certainly never made that mistake again. The best websites for following what a celebrity has worn are WireImage.com, GettyImages.com, and PRPhotos.com. If you search a celebrity's name on these sites, you'll see what he or she wore to all the recent red carpet events and movie premieres.

BRINGING IT ALL BACK HOME

You may not face the issue of choosing between A-, B-, and C-list celebrities, but even in your community, individuals have different levels of celebrity. If you live in a small town and are considering applying these techniques locally, you might wonder how to find your own influencers and VIPs. My suggestion is to start by reading local newspapers and magazines. I keep a file and tear out articles on people and events that might be of interest to a client down the road. Take time to introduce yourself to every local VIP and influencer you think can help expand awareness of your brand. If you can afford it, give out free product to make the individual feel like even more of a VIP.

Editors of local media are another group to target; they inspire readers on a daily basis. Seek out two editors that you think can spark your own creativity and business. Editors are messengers of information and should be considered influencers no matter what city or town you live in.

If your merchandise lends itself to sports, you must connect with every local coach and top athlete within driving distance. Depending on your demographic, you might consider athletes who played sports professionally and still live in your city. Many still maintain connections and are visible through various charitable efforts.

Politicians, city council, and other people you read about consistently in the local news are always important. They have strong ties to the community and can help bring your message to more people.

Even friends with large networks can give a product a big boost, as Jean Derby discovered. Jean describes herself as a girl with a sewing machine and a desire to stay at home with her kids. Her website, www .MadeByJeanDerby.com, offers everything from cloth diapers and guitar straps to jewelry and clothing. "I enjoy creating beauty out of what would otherwise be discarded," she says. Her business took off when she sent her own gifts to friends at Christmas. Her friends helped spread the word, and now she is selling internationally to customers in Hong Kong, Italy, and the United Kingdom.

Learning the Landscape

- Realize that there are different tiers of celebrities, but don't necessarily limit your placement campaign to one tier.
- Stay up to date on what celebrities are doing by reading entertainment industry websites and publications.
- Be prepared to devote a sizeable budget to any product placement campaign while understanding that the results are not certain, and that you might only get a minor celebrity.
- Understand that new categories of celebrity, such as reality TV celebrities, appear with regularity and might offer great opportunities for your product.
- Realize that there are different levels of celebrities even in local markets.

CHAPTER 3

TIERS *of* EVENTS

"I wasn't naked; I was completely covered by a blue spotlight." —GYPSY ROSE LEE

Like the tiers of celebrity, there are tiers of events—and not all of them will benefit your product.

I've met quite a few celebrities who *need* to be in the spotlight at a top-tier event; it's like a drug for them. If they don't stay in the spotlight, they'll disappear—not a pretty picture for those whose income is hinged to first-name status. Those are the celebrities who will get your product seen. Like them or not, they are the *best* celebrities for getting your merchandise noticed. They're always on the lookout for a red, green, blue, or any hue carpet to strut down, hoping their photo will land in a weekly tabloid. This means opportunities for you and your brand.

Then there are a whole other group of celebrities who prefer to hide unless they are promoting a project. These are an elite cluster of stars like George Clooney, Julia Roberts, Angelina Jolie, and so on. You just don't see them in front of cameras or attending many events unless it is for a charity

The stunning Charlize Theron at the Golden Globes.

Photo by Associated Press

they support. With these more reclusive celebrities, you'll have to do a lot of research and have great timing and connections to have them seen at any type of event with your product.

> *"I've heard people make comments like 'You don't really want to be in the tabloids, but you need to be for your career.' They believe it's actually important. It's not. It's ugly . . . People say, 'That's your job.' It really isn't, actually. It's not my job to go out there and make an ass out of myself."*
> —CHARLIZE THERON, BRITISH GQ, JULY 2008

WORKING *with the* GATEKEEPERS

If you're hoping to get celebrities to notice or wear your product at an event, you'll have to learn to work with their gatekeepers. Many celebrities employ publicists to help them maintain their star status and keep them in front of the cameras and media. Publicists assist them in promoting a new film or TV project, book them on talk shows, schedule photo shoots, and arrange (along with movie studios) the glamorous premieres they attend for themselves or other celebrities.

At Film Fashion, I would frequently get calls from celebrity publicists throwing out names of their young celeb clients, hoping for a front-row seat at a fashion show. Producing a fashion show includes choosing people to sit in the "front of house" section, which might sound thrilling, but for me it was also a serious job: I needed to fill those seats with influential people, and I had to get the gatekeepers to understand why my event was a perfect fit for their star. Those celebrity publicists and I both shared a common goal of trying to get our clients noticed. I tried to fill my front row with mainly important fashion editors and then sprinkle in a few well-known celebrities. As I filled the section, publicists tried to convince me that their up-and-coming stars were just one film away from stardom. I was always happy when I confirmed a great celebrity for an envied front-row seat, but at the same time, I dreaded the elbows and body slams necessary to get the celeb to his or her seat before show time.

> *"Press junkets have always been a hard job because none of the designers actually get credited. No one actually says 'I'm wearing this [designer]' at a press junket. The red carpet and magazine editorials are usually good because the designer's name gets mentioned, thanks to magazines like* InStyle *and* Us, *networks like* E!, *and shows like* Entertainment Tonight. *"*
> —PHILLIP BLOCH, HOLLYWOOD FASHION STYLIST

HOLLYWOOD'S BIGGEST NIGHTS

For a fashion designer, the Academy Awards are the holy grail of celebrity marketing. The red carpet and photos that follow that event are shown all over the world. The broadcast is watched by approximately 44 million television viewers domestically and is seen in 150 countries internationally—and then, of course, all the photos are viewed on the Internet. Obviously, this kind of free advertising can make a large impression and increase sales overnight.

The Oscars take place in February or March, but for me, the campaign to determine who will be attending this prestigious event starts right after Christmas. I've placed many fashion designers and fashion products on Oscar winners and Oscar nominees and enjoyed the exposure my clients experienced along with them. In the beginning, this process was fun and exciting for the smaller players, but over the years, I've seen it change as the large fashion houses, which have immense marketing budgets, push out the smaller fashion designers. These large fashion houses started to view pay-ing a celebrity to wear their product as a part of their marketing budget—knowing they were almost guaranteed worldwide press.

"I am a believer and practitioner of doing my homework well in advance. For the Oscars, I have always had designers sketch options for my clients at least three months in advance. Then, the process of eliminating options and creating the top three gown choices begins. Sometimes, the Oscar choice has been chosen directly from the runway, but it still has to be custom-made for my client." —STYLIST AND DESIGNER FATI PARSIA, WHO HAS STYLED CATHERINE ZETA-JONES FOR THE OSCARS

I view working on the Oscars for my clients as something similar to what campaigning for the presidency of the United States must feel like. If a celebrity feels he or she has a shot at being nominated for an Oscar, the celeb needs to get in front of the voters in the Academy of Motion Picture Arts and Sciences, which has approximately six thousand active and life members. This means boundless opportunities for your brand to partner up with a star because there are so many events leading up to the Oscars.

In early 2010, Sandra Bullock attended the Santa Barbara International Film Festival for *The Blind Side*, and while other Oscar nominees might have taken a day off after the event, Sandra continued by stopping by *The Late Show with David Letterman* in New York City. Sandra's Oscar cam-paign also included appearances at the Golden Globes, the Screen Actors Guild Awards, the Critics' Choice Awards, and a multitude of other events leading up to the Academy Awards. Sandra even went so far as to attend the Razzie Awards to pick up her award for *worst* actress for a role in *All About Steve*, another film released that same year. There were a multitude of eyes on her and her wardrobe at each and every one of those events.

If you've set your sights on the Oscars and want to connect with a celebrity during an Academy Awards campaign, here are a few quick tips:

- Start at the grassroots level. If you are able to work with a celebrity on a local event, this can open the door to showing the individual goods for bigger, more important events.

- Do research to find out which celebrities are likely to attend the Academy Awards.

- Consider a lesser cast member of a nominated or likely-to-be-nominated film. The person might not get a nomination, but will attend as part of a nominated film.

- Look into various events each person will attend during his or her campaign.

I was always pleasantly surprised by creative ideas I witnessed from some unlikely fashion brands at the Oscars. Especially when considering a top-tier event like a huge award show, you have to take into account the celebrity's attitude toward the personal image he or she wishes to project. Of course, the harder part is hoping the star will connect to your product. I am constantly reminded that fashion—clothing and accessories—are personal. It's hard to blame a celebrity for turning down a dress—even a free one—if it's something she just can't picture herself wearing. Finding a good fit for your brand is important; otherwise, you might jump through hoops only to be turned down or end up working with a celebrity who doesn't connect with your core customers as she accepts her award.

"We have seen companies like Lee Jeans at the Academy Awards providing denim caps to the fans in the bleachers. I recall GM's 'TEN' fashion shows in Hollywood, which thrived on Oscar hype. And Hush Puppies were big for Forrest Gump." —TOM JULIAN, FOUNDER OF THE TOM JULIAN GROUP, A BRAND CONSULTANCY, AND STYLE EXPERT FOR OSCAR .COM, THE OFFICIAL WEBSITE FOR THE ACADEMY AWARDS

Academy Award nominee Taraji Henson
looking radiant on the red carpet.

Photo by PR Photos

Other huge red carpet events to consider are

- the Golden Globes (16.9 million viewers)
- the Emmy Awards (13.5 million viewers)
- the Tony Awards (7 million viewers)
- the People's Choice Awards (10.8 million viewers)
- the Screen Actors Guild Awards (13.5 million viewers)
- the Grammy Awards (25.8 million viewers)
- the Kids' Choice Awards (7.6 viewers)
- the Academy of Country Music Awards (41.3 million viewers)
- the Teen Choice Awards (5.7 million viewers)
- the MTV Movie Awards (16.4 million viewers)

This list is just a small sampling of the countless award shows that draw a big viewership. It's simple to understand why celebrities attend all these award shows and why they have become a tremendous way to market and expose product. Since there is a red carpet event just about every weekend, there is no need to get discouraged if you can't connect to a star or singer for one of these prestigious events. Rest assured that there's always another red carpet coming up.

THE INTERNATIONAL WORLD *of* FILM FESTIVALS

There are many star-studded film festivals that occur throughout the world, each of which represents a unique opportunity for celebrity marketing. Unlike award shows, these festivals often last well over a week, making them important "gets" for any celebrity marketer. You can visit FilmFestivals.com to read more about the locale and genre of most festivals.

Utah's Sundance Film Festival has become a marketing dream for many. Imagine ski chalets stocked with products like sunglasses, vodka, and luxury watches—all of which are seen by celebrities, media, producers, and directors. Each year, I researched the films that would be shown at Sundance and the celebrities who would be attending. Then, I would compile a targeted list of people to whom I planned to distribute winter coats by Kenneth Cole. Armed with images of the trendy coats Kenneth Cole had offered up that year, I attacked my list with gusto.

The Cannes Film Festival in France might be about the business of buying, selling, and distributing films, but for me, it's about fashion product placement and the business of putting gowns and expensive jewelry on celebrities. There is a red carpet on each of the festival's thirteen nights, with photos splashed around the world. Dior, Chanel, Armani, Versace, Fendi, Dolce & Gabbana, Alberta Ferretti, Roberto Cavalli, Emilio Pucci, Yves Saint Laurent, and my clients Lanvin, Chopard, and Swarovski all compete for the prize of dressing international stars and starlets.

For the Cannes premiere of *Moulin Rouge*, Swarovski sprinkled clear crystals all over the red carpet, making the ground shine like diamonds. This promotion caught the attention of the press, who repeatedly mentioned that Swarovski had provided the crystals on the carpet, as well as for the elaborate costumes of Nicole Kidman—creating a bigger story than just the crystals sprinkled under the feet of the stars.

Chopard's co-president and designer, Caroline Gruosi-Scheufele, has been a longtime supporter of the cinematic arts. Twelve years ago, Ms. Gruosi-Scheufele was asked to redesign the prestigious Palme d'Or Award—the highest prize awarded to competing films at Cannes. The award she designed includes a palm made of twenty-four-carat gold, hand-cast into a wax mold, and attached to a single piece of cut crystal. The award is presented in a case of blue Morocco leather. Clearly, the honor of designing the award was a beneficial marketing tool for the luxury jewelry company. Each year, Chopard provides jewelry to top actresses who attend Cannes, including Marion Cotillard and Penelope Cruz.

Relationships Chopard makes at the film festival often continue on to numerous award shows and even movies. For example, the company collaborated with costume designer Colleen Atwood on the film *Nine* to create pieces for the characters played by Nicole Kidman, Marion Cotillard, and Kate Hudson.

For many years, Budweiser brought a spectacular yacht to the Cannes Film Festival to host daily parties. Sharon Stone and Adrien Brody were some of the guests on the "beer boat." Laurane C. Sheehan, a respected public relations professional, said:

> Handling A-listers is an art. I brought Adrien [Brody] into the Anheuser-Busch fold before his Oscar, during a meteoric rise in his career. At Cannes, it was my job to make sure he felt comfortable staying on the AB yacht. Star-handling is a time-honored skill, and the celebrities' representatives trust the handler's instincts for their other clients. Being a liaison between corporate looky-loos and A-list celebrities means keeping both happy and protected!

Movie premieres are the most frequent type of event you'll come across, from the biggest summer blockbuster films, to holiday and dramatic movies with potential to win awards. Movie premieres are endless and held almost every weekend on both the West and East Coasts. Again, one of the most useful websites I know to find out about everything and everyone in entertainment is IMDb.com. There, you can learn about upcoming movie premieres to map out your own strategy and celebrities to target.

One of the best red carpet promotion ideas I came across was the "million-dollar shoes," designed by international high-end shoe company Stuart Weitzman. Starting in 2002, Mr. Weitzman created a pair of one-of-a-kind diamond shoes worn by an Oscar nominee to the Academy Awards, creating worldwide publicity. Although Alison Krauss's Oscar-nominated song for *Cold Mountain* didn't win Best Song, her fortunate feet got the red carpet treatment: She got to wear shoes valued at more than two million dollars. When Mr. Weitzman arrived in Los Angeles the week before the Oscars with the dazzling, irreplaceable shoes, the press lined up because the idea was a press magnet.

Alison Krauss in Stuart Weitzman's million-dollar shoes.

AP Photo/Amy Sancetta

Stuart Weitzman and his million-dollar shoes.

The perception of being the celebrity selected to wear the shoes each year was one of glamour and intrigue, as we all anticipated who would be chosen. However, all good ideas come to an end, and such was the case for the million-dollar shoes. Evidently, it got harder for the brand to find a celebrity to wear the shoes. Many of the bold-faced names attending the Oscars felt the concept worked to promote Stuart Weitzman, but didn't reflect well on them. Mr. Weitzman even upped the ante by offering to make a donation to a celebrity's charity of choice, but still the idea didn't have its previous appeal. Take that as a lesson: You should always know when to fold before a good idea goes bad and becomes a publicity stunt gone wrong.

Still, the campaign was so successful that I stopped reading bylines about it on a Google search after twenty-five pages. Did Mr. Weitzman get his money's worth? You bet!

MAKING THE MOST
of PRODUCT PLACEMENT

Films, TV shows, and music videos are part of another type of "event" in which you can aim to have products featured. This type of embedded marketing, which is what most people mean when they use the term *product placement*, occurs when a branded product or service is featured in a media production, often worked into the storyline. The appearance is almost never disclosed as an advertisement.

One of the best examples of product placement in full action is the modern James Bond film. Every product clearly seen, from the sleek automobile Bond drives to the watch he wears, is a form of product placement. In some cases, product placement can be very subtle, ranging from a logo on a shopping bag to the name on a tube of toothpaste glimpsed in a character's bathroom.

Product placement can be paid for in a variety of ways—sometimes through fees, bartering, or monthly service charges for full-blown product placement agencies. A majority of products end up in films and TV shows without paying; instead, some brands opt to provide loads of merchandise free of charge to the producers. Two successes that come to mind are Reese's Pieces in *E.T.* and, more recently, the BMW Mini Coopers gone wild in the 2003 remake of *The Italian Job*. According to Abram Sauer, writing for BrandChannel.com, Clos Du Val wine has made one hundred appearances in film and TV by sending directors free cases. "Whether or not these placements directly boost sales is hard to determine," writes Sauer, "but the winery has reported 50 percent higher sales over last year."

My expertise is in using the red carpet for fashion and accessory brands, but I did help some clients place their product in TV and films. I had to examine each request with my clients and determine whether the cost outweighed the risk—it was always possible that the scene with my client's product (or the entire movie) would end up on the cutting room floor.

When the producers of *The Devil Wears Prada* came calling to ask if any high-end couture clients would lend them film of their fashion shows for a particular scene, Georges Chakra quickly agreed. Watch closely as Meryl Streep visits Paris as the fashion editor of *Runway Magazine*. If you blink, you might miss it, but this little hit helped open doors for Georges. With your own research into costume designers, prop masters, and stylists, and some consistency, you will get your own breakthrough. I had very few clients who had the budget to pay for a placement in a film, but I did often have the connections to help them. I read every entertainment magazine I can get my hands on, and when I hear about something that might be a good fit for a client, I make the calls.

There haven't been a lot of fashion films made—which is why I usually look elsewhere to get the most exposure for clients. I found that the costume designers for *Entertainment Tonight, Access Hollywood, The Insider,* and other entertainment shows were usually very agreeable to bartering exposure for product. Billy Bush might not be as big an influencer as, say, an actor playing James Bond, but his show is seen by millions of fashion-conscious viewers each week, and those impressions can add up.

HOLLYWOOD GLITZ *at* HOME

Can't get to Hollywood? How about stealing a few ideas from La La Land and using them in your local market? Remember that tire shop in St. Louis I mentioned in the introduction? Hardly a candidate for showing up on the red carpet, right? Well, what if that shop created its own red carpet event and gave it some Hollywood flair?

Riding the success of the movie *Twilight*, Nordstrom sold cardboard cutouts of the movie's characters and hosted Twilight Takeover parties featuring a makeup line called Luna Twilight, which sells vampire-themed cosmetics—including Twilight Venom lipstick and Mortal Glow Blushing Crème. Our St. Louis tire shop could take Nordstrom's idea and reinvent it by offering up Twilight tire deals, redeemed at dusk by Twilight-character look-alikes. Or, the shop could have the staff dress up as undead heart-throbs and serve blood-colored beverages to customers. Almost any small business can look to Hollywood marketing experts to find inspiration and get ideas for creating small-scale events.

Even huge brands look to intimate events to connect with local clients. In 2010, Louis Vuitton kicked off its Salons de Louis Vuitton series (during which the brand invites top clients and their friends to have an audience with influential artists) by hosting a dinner with Mikhail Baryshnikov. The surprise treat was a performance by nineteen-year-old Kate Davis, a jazz bassist and singer from Portland, Oregon, who was discovered by Baryshnikov. This idea is something that can be reinvented in Anytown, USA. Kick off your own salon, inviting your friends and a special VIP from your own town. Within a few months, your dinners will be the hot ticket, and you will have created a buzz around your name, product, or service. As long as you can mix up the guest list and include someone a little unexpected, you'll have a great party.

KEEP YOUR FOCUS *on the* CELEBRITY

No matter what the level of event you're working with, remember that the key thing is your relationship with the celebrity. These connections will provide you with priceless long-term benefits, especially when it comes to celebrity marketing.

I learned that there is a difference between the "no" and "maybe" response you'll hear from celebrities and their support teams when you approach them with different events. If I got a definite no from a celebrity, I certainly don't want to stalk the person and risk building a relationship in the future. However, if I believe the no was perhaps a maybe, then I will always look for another event or idea to approach the celebrity about again.

Ellen DeGeneres's costume designer frequently visited Film Fashion looking for just the right outfits for Ellen and partner Portia de Rossi to wear to events. Both of these women have very specific tastes, so it wasn't often that she found something to their liking among the offerings from my clients. But by keeping the door open, the costume designer frequently shared opportunities where I might tie in a client with Ellen's talk show. Ellen's "Twelve Days of Giveaways" is an annual event in which she gifts her guests leading up to Christmas. Swarovski enjoyed tremendous exposure one Christmas on an item it donated while millions of people watched. It might not have been a top-tier event on the level of the Oscars, but it nevertheless had a tremendous impact on Ellen's core viewership.

Learning the Landscape

- There are Hollywood events every week—premieres, award shows, and film festivals. Not all events are right for your brand, garner media attention, or host your target list of celebrities, so choose wisely.

- Think ahead! Don't wait until a few days before an event to try to make connections.

- Don't discount reality stars or lower-caste celebrities. You might like the exposure they can offer through all the events they attend to promote themselves.

- Don't go all out for a huge event and neglect all other opportunities. A continuous stream of events that showcase your product in the best light is your ultimate marketing goal.

- Shooting for the A-list stars? Make sure they have a film or charity event to promote so they'll actually have somewhere to appear with your product. Be on the lookout for films, events, and causes that might align your interests with the celebrity's. (We'll talk more about charities in chapter 11.)

CHAPTER 4

PERSISTENCE
and CHANGE

The fashion industry goes into high alert with each change of weather and season. In this cyclical business, you work all year round to transform last year's flavor of design, textures, fabrics, and colors into a new must-have item that will draw buyers to retail stores. But it's not just fashion that changes; the way red carpet marketing works is constantly adapting as well.

In the beginning of celebrity marketing, some designers recognized the changing dynamics of the industry and forged ahead into new territory. Making a call and saying "Mr. Armani would love to dress you" was all it took to have the most recognizable stars on board. As the field evolved, designers began handpicking celebrities to represent them—among Armani's choices were Jodie Foster and Michelle Pfeiffer. In exchange for Armani product, they would wear the designer's wares for red carpet appearances. This arrangement meant they were walking around wearing the brand every day, and it cost the designer very little. The celebrities became so known for the brands they worked with that even if they weren't wearing the designer's clothing, people thought they were.

"I'm wearing a Giorgio Armani Suit.
He's been very supportive." — MAD MEN
STAR JON HAMM, AT A *DETAILS* PARTY

These days, celebrity dressing is a two-way street. If the right celebrity wears a designer's dress, it can result in hundreds, thousands, or even millions of dollars in publicity with little investment. For the celebrity, it's also a win because not only does she have something wonderful to wear, but she also doesn't have to pay for an outfit she can never wear again. (Normal folks might wear a favorite outfit many times, but a celebrity will be ridiculed in the celebrity weeklies for the repetition.)

What this means for you is that if you're persistent enough, there are ample opportunities to work with all kinds of celebrities. It's about finding the right celebrity—one who embodies your brand and whom the media will want to write about—and then working hard to find the right avenue for getting your product into the person's hands. It's about perseverance, which might mean taking a non-established route to your placement objective and goals.

Persistence is the key quality you need to profit from celebrity marketing, whether you're pitching chewing gum or a luxury fashion line. Fashion is fickle, and marketing to celebrities is not the right niche for everyone, but I enjoyed the challenge. Don't give up after the first try. You might need to change your strategy as you go along, and that could include modifying your list of celebrities, the events you target, and the paths you take to get to the stars. If you have the ability to persist through setbacks and cope with changes in the industry, you'll dramatically increase your chances for success.

UNDER THE INFLUENCE

Jill Boehler—a speech pathologist turned fashion entrepreneur—got her big break through a combination of a unique idea and an incredible amount of persistence. Boehler designed a wrap—the Chilly Jilly—that is soft, lightweight, and small enough to keep in your purse. It provides plenty of warmth and can double as a sarong at the beach or scarf on a cold winter day. Boehler pinned her hopes on getting the wrap in the hands of Oprah Winfrey for a mention from the powerful talk show diva—a lofty goal indeed. But Boehler's persistence paid off in a big way. She called and e-mailed Oprah's show and magazine every day for six months until she finally caught a producer's interest. Her determination to succeed undoubtedly impressed those producers, who were probably used to a few phone calls before the promoter gave up.

Getting in touch with an actor through his or her management or publicist can be daunting, especially with the A-list actors. Years ago, actresses were under contract to one studio that took care of everything. But there's no longer one single, dedicated, studio-employed costumer—think Edith Head in the forties, fifties, and sixties—who dresses stars for every occasion and maintains their hair, makeup, and wardrobe. Now, actors and performers get their clothes and accessories from many different sources, and it takes a lot of work and ingenuity to get noticed. Here's where taking the road less traveled and trying a different approach might be your path to a star.

For instance, you don't necessarily have to take the typical route of going through the star's publicist. Costume designers for movies and TV are always interested in finding new sources for projects they are working on. They work under tight budgets and are open to finding a way of getting interesting, fun products to incorporate into a film or TV series. Look to a costume designer or a set decorator for interest in your product and an introduction to the actors and "influencers" on the set, like producers and directors. Any product enthusiastically endorsed by a costume designer or other influencer is more likely to get an actor's attention.

"OUT *of* OPTIONS, BUT NOT IDEAS"

Kenneth Cole tells a great story in his book, *Footnotes*, about his own start in the business. He writes: "The footwear industry, like most, has 'market weeks'—days when the industry comes together to view its options. Buyers would converge at the Hilton Hotel to see what more than 1,100 small- to medium-sized footwear companies have to offer." Since Kenneth couldn't afford to show his product in the hotel, or to set up a showroom in the blocks surrounding the hotel, as the bigger shoe companies did, he followed his instincts and had a very unique idea. "I was out of options, but not ideas," he writes. "On a whim, I called a friend in the trucking business and asked to borrow one of his trailers to park it on 56th Street and Sixth Avenue, two blocks from the Hilton and in front of a fancy shoe building. 'Sure, but good luck getting permission,' he said. 'This is New York. You can't park a bicycle there for four minutes, let alone a truck for four days.'"

Showing his entrepreneurial strategies early in life, Kenneth called Mayor Koch's office and asked about getting a permit to park a trailer truck on the street. The city office explained that it only made exceptions for city utility trucks and sometimes movie production companies. Kenneth ran to a stationery store and quickly printed up new letterhead, changing the company name from "Kenneth Cole, Inc." to "Kenneth Cole Productions." The next day, letterhead in hand, Kenneth applied for a permit to shoot a full-length motion picture entitled *The Birth of a Shoe Company*. With Kenneth Cole Productions printed on the side of the truck, he rented movie cameras (sometimes with film) and hired models to play actresses. The city even supplied two policemen. Curiosity brought every important buyer to the trailer, and the resourceful designer sold forty thousand pairs of shoes in three and a half days. As Kenneth says, "the best solution is not always the most expensive, but usually the most creative."

Sometimes, brands need to be creative in selecting partners—even if the partner seems out of reach. Most people don't associate Payless ShoeSource with high fashion, and it certainly took some determination and out-of-the-box thinking for the discount retailer to end up on the red carpet. But Payless got there, by forging a relationship with Patricia Field, costume designer for *Sex and the City*, when she was nominated for an Oscar in 2006 for *The Devil Wears Prada*. Patricia had been key in playing up the importance of footwear in fashion; both she and Sarah Jessica Parker were obsessed with shoes. Patricia designed an original pair of shoes for Payless as part of the "Red Carpet Collection by Patricia Field" and wore them to the big event. Payless knew that tying their heels to Patricia, an in-demand costume designer for big fashion movies, just might help them walk through Hollywood's golden door and into a glossy Patricia Field project.

GOING FUR-THER

Jaclyn Sharp, founder of the faux-fur fashion brand Imposter and newcomer to the world of celebrity marketing, stuck persistently with her intuition that working with celebrities would help launch her business, despite initial negative feedback. It wasn't easy to convince celebrities to go faux over real fur, but finally, after many tries, Jaclyn (with Film Fashion's help) got some great celebrities interested. Her first wish list included Angelina Jolie, Blake Lively, Scarlett Johansson, Charlize Theron, Heidi Klum, Jessica Biel, Kim Kardashian, Megan Fox, Sienna Miller, and Kate Hudson. None of these actresses expressed interest in wearing the faux-chinchilla vest, so she reexamined her list and we started over. "Celebrities start almost all trends in fashion, and celebrities at the top of their industry can make all the difference," says Jaclyn. Another round of outreach sparked the interest of animal lovers Carrie Underwood, Emmy Rossum, Dakota Fanning,

Sarah Jessica Parker in faux-fur by Imposter.

Sarah Jessica Parker, and Angie Harmon. "Most of the celebrities are people that care a lot about animals. Stars who risk the wrath of PETA and insist on stepping out in real fur perhaps just need a little educating," said Jaclyn. Had she stopped after a few rebuffs, she wouldn't be where she is today.

Photos Courtesy of Imposter

Imposter's faux-chinchilla vest.

Jaclyn Sharp, founder of
faux-fur company Imposter.

A PICTURE IS WORTH
A THOUSAND WORDS

When Nikon hired me to promote its new instant camera, Coolpix, on the red carpet, I had to use an unusual approach to make the promotion effective. This sounded like a fun project, and we all agreed it would be great to have celebrities carry the cameras while strutting on the carpet, where they could turn the camera on their friends and the ever-present paparazzi. But how could I make that happen? I was given some sample cameras to gift but needed to be prudent: There was no guarantee that a celebrity would carry the camera to the carpet once I gave it to him or her.

Rather than going the usual route and directly approaching a celebrity, I took the idea to E! network. Why? Because I had a limited number of cameras to gift, and no guarantee of any press or coverage. I offered up the Coolpix cameras as an on-air gift whenever a celebrity walked over to speak with Joan and Melissa Rivers. E! loved this idea, especially because Joan was a loose cannon and some celebrities were nervous to speak with her because they didn't know what she might ask or say. The executives thought the camera display might lure over a few nervous celebrities to Joan and Melissa's station on the red carpet.

Even designers must sometimes devise a creative approach to secure successful promotion of their clothing. Jeremy Piven, a lead actor in *Entourage,* was one of the first celebrities to embrace Domenico Vacca's Italian suiting. Once the menswear designer had the star in his threads, Vacca decided his clothing needed a starring role in the show, too. How did he make it happen? Word of mouth about the clothing from Piven, along with an offer to gift a tuxedo to the show's writer/producer, was the first attempt to barter the designer's clothing into the script. The writer/producer was certainly intrigued by the idea. Once he fell in love with Vacca's tailored clothing, he presented his idea to write a special scene in the Entourage script. He offered to film "the boys" of *Entourage* walking into a Domenico Vacca store in exchange for the luxurious tuxedo. A deal was struck, and Vacca himself did the fitting for the scene.

BE PREPARED *for* CHANGE, EVEN *at the* BEGINNING

When I launched Film Fashion, I didn't have a client for six months. I used most of my savings by traveling to New York and Europe for meetings. Everyone I met with loved the idea of Film Fashion, but didn't quite understand it. I was starting to panic and thought about getting another job. But I kept at it until I got a call from the people at Ralph Lauren: "We're launching a line of women's gowns and we're going to hire you to help us get the gowns on celebrities for the Oscars."

I was thrilled. Ralph Lauren is great, and I figured this would be a slam dunk—that is, until I saw photographs of the collection I was to promote. The dresses were very simple—pretty much slip gowns—in crayon colors: yellow, fuchsia, and electric blue. I realized this was going to be a tough project. I had picked up tips from the best costume designers and stylists in the business, so I knew crayon colors were not camera-friendly and that on the biggest night in Hollywood, a mere slip dress would not be considered memorable fashion. Plus, Lauren insisted that anyone wearing one of his gowns also wear Ralph Lauren from head to toe. They had to wear Ralph Lauren shoes, handbags, and jewelry, and the designer would even make suggestions for their hairstyles and make-up. Clearly, that left no room for the actor's individual style.

Well, I was not successful. None of my contacts were interested. A few weeks before the Oscars, it was time to switch my strategy. Instead of approaching the women, I tried to dress men in Lauren's classic tuxedos. I had failed Lauren's test, but reaching out to the men was better than nothing, and I hoped Lauren's PR staff might applaud my last-ditch efforts. On the night of the Academy Awards, Denzel Washington, who's considered a snappy dresser, wore a Ralph Lauren tuxedo. I may have failed on my original mission, but I was prepared to be flexible, and I ended up getting Ralph Lauren on the red carpet.

Finding the perfect chemistry between product and celebrity can take a significant amount of work. Let's say you have a bicycle company and decide a celebrity photographed riding your hot pink cycle will skyrocket sales of your bike. The photo of this celebrity on your website will help you show how cool the bike is. You send photos of the bike out to your target list of stars with no luck. What's your next step?

You could come up with another list of celebrities and try again, which is certainly an example of the persistence you will need to jump into celebrity marketing. However, I would probably recommend researching other avenues for getting exposure for that hot pink bike and looking at another way to make an inroad to Hollywood. Investigate which stars ride bikes for fun with their families (and get photographed). Seek out events that might involve biking, like the Coachella music festival in Indio, California. Make a list of TV shows where a character might ride a bike in a scene. Contact music companies to see if any rock bands are filming a scene involving a bike. Keep building a list with crazy ideas and then start dialing the phone. I can't promise you'll hit it out of the park, but I can guarantee you'll start building your list of contacts. The professionals will ask you to send them photos with your contact info, and they'll file your information. Your persistence will pay off. Just think about what your target demographic likes to do. Don't let yourself be confined by the same old demographic boundaries, either: Many thirteen-year-olds now think they're twenty-five—it's all about the mind-set. Today's customer does everything—so you have to cast a wider net.

The bottom line is that you need to be flexible when working with celebrities. They are real people, in spite of the mega-salaries they command and the lifestyles they lead. Like real people, they enjoy receiving things for free or having the chance to borrow rather than buy. Who wouldn't like a closet to dip into whenever you need something? The road to making this happen can run smoothly or take a few detours.

Harrison Ford once said, "We all have big changes in our lives that are more or less a second chance." Think of changes in the industry as new chances or opportunities to do something new or pioneering—even if the change at first seems like a terrible development.

If you're prepared for change, you should also be prepared for a few second chances . . .

Learning the Landscape

- Persistence will be the key to your success. Don't give up; give it another try.
- There are no clear paths into Hollywood except creativity.
- Consider non-established routes and ideas. Something that hasn't been tried before is something that might lead to your own box-office success.
- Be flexible, and try to capture success even if it's not what you originally envisioned.

CHAPTER 5

MAGAZINES, TELEVISION, *and the* POWER *of the* INTERNET

The early days of celebrity marketing were an uncomplicated time. But change is inevitable, and it came swiftly in the field of celebrity marketing when everyone realized that celebrities had become walking billboards.

For decades, the public has been fascinated by what movie stars wear, and people frequently have a strong desire to emulate a certain style they see in the movies. The cinema was really the first place where stars began to exert a strong influence on the consuming public. One of the earliest examples is a dress created by costume designer Adrian for Joan Crawford in the film *Letty Lynton*. The dress he created had padded shoulders to camouflage Crawford's broad shoulders, setting off a national craze for shoulder pads. Adrian explained the phenomenon this way: "Thousands of women are impelled to copy her, not only because they think they can look like her, but because they hope they can achieve the positive quality that is her great attraction." Thus, Joan Crawford was one of the original movie stars who served as a fashion model to viewers.

Joan Crawford in the Adrian dress that became a
sensation after the release of Letty Lynton.

*"The media is obsessed with celebrities, what they wear,
and what bag they carry—whether it be at the
Academy Awards or to grab a latte. My friend Prabal
Garung launched a collection of mostly cocktail dresses
that Rachel Zoe put Demi Moore in twice within a
ninety-day period. His star skyrocketed from this
exposure and took him from a young designer with
industry-based notoriety to a red-carpet must-have."*
— BILLY DALEY, WORLDWIDE DIRECTOR
OF MEDIA AND SPECIAL EVENTS / U.S.
COMMUNICATIONS DIRECTOR, BOTTEGA
VENETA (FORMERLY OF MICHAEL KORS)

The men of movies could also create a stir in setting trends. Clark Gable's bare chest in the 1934 film *It Happened One Night* caused a recession in the men's underwear industry. Marlon Brando and James Dean's casual T-shirt look is still studied and updated in fashion, and even among today's stars.

The list of fashion trends influenced by characters is long: Steve McQueen's leather jacket, Audrey Hepburn's little black dress, John Travolta's white suit in *Saturday Night Fever*, Diane Keaton's menswear for women in *Annie Hall*, Ali MacGraw's knit hats in *Love Story*, and so on.

But, of course, the public's fascination with popular stars isn't limited to clothing seen in movies. Elvis Presley and the Beatles changed how men wore their hair. Teen idol Justin Bieber's hairstyle could be considered an updated Beatles''do.

Trends like these slowly trickled into the culture, and some built momentum in the public eye. As time passed, more and more fashion editors from newspapers and magazines wrote about these trends, and retail stores supported them.

In the years after I started Film Fashion, I worked alongside the designer, stylist, and star, hoping a look would catch the public's attention, but there

Audrey Hepburn's distinctive black-dress-and-pearls look.

wasn't an organized fashion-media machine like there is today. *InStyle* was the closest thing to it, and it was my bible—the magazine offered articles about beauty, fashion, and celebrity lifestyles. My clients had really made it if one of their products, worn by a celebrity of note, made the pages of the glossy, star-studded magazine.

Although the entire fashion industry has changed even more in recent times with the rise of celebrity TV shows and the Internet revolution, magazines are still a powerful force for product placement. For the time being at least, consumers still enjoy viewing fashion items in the high-gloss photos of printed magazines.

Steve McQueen wearing his influential leather jacket.

Photo Courtesy of MGM Stills Department

THE CONTINUED POPULARITY
of MAGAZINES

The American public has an insatiable appetite for anything celebrity related—one need only visit a newsstand to see racks of magazines, ranging from *People* and *Us Weekly* to *In Touch Weekly* and *Star*, promoting celebrities and what they wear. *InStyle* and *People* have both increased profits for parent company Time Warner by publishing special "Style Watch" and fashion how-to editions that are produced in addition to the magazines' regular issues. The special edition issues can reach over 500,000 people, and celebrities and what they're wearing figure very prominently in them.

People caught the fashion world's attention when readership started climbing to over three million, and *Us Weekly* came in second at almost two million. Even *Star*, *In Touch Weekly*, and other newcomers to the world of weekly celebrity publications started with impressive numbers. It was easy to dismiss the gossip-filled *National Enquirer*, but when the publication started a fashion page and announced a circulation of over 1.5 million, all of us in the industry took notice. As common as it was to send out a press release about a fashion product, it was still uncommon in the fashion world to target newspapers, magazines, and Internet sites with descriptions of what celebrities wore. Anna Wintour and *Vogue* started putting celebrities on the cover, recognizing that celebs sell magazines, along with merchandise they wear to events and in their personal lives. "The bottom line is celebrities sell much better," said Wintour, according to Dana Thomas's book *Deluxe* (Penguin, 2007).

With over 30 percent of the 2,400 U.S. magazine pages featuring celebrities, I've made a career for myself and helped jump-start brand and product visibility by having designers' products seen on celebrities in these magazines, which continue to boom even with so many people on the Internet. In fact, I see the Internet not as a threat to magazines, but as an incredible supplement: With some websites reaching almost four million unique visitors per month, consumers are one click away from a sale.

"The celebrity factor generates huge media coverage and thus directly influences the consumer's behavior. Any designer's brand that is associated with a celebrity can receive this kind of recognition." –GEORGES CHAKRA

THE BRITNEY EFFECT

I recognized that the public's fascination with what celebrities wore was moving at a breakneck pace when pop princess Britney Spears surprised the world with her marriage to Kevin Federline and the news was printed in every celebrity weekly. Though Britney's popularity may have waned a bit since her heyday, the story of her wedding gown—and the press it got its designer—is still a fantastic illustration of the power of celebrity reporting on the Web and in magazines, and how it can change someone's business.

My client Monique Lhuillier, at the time still a relatively unknown wedding gown designer, was chosen as the lucky designer of the gown. We had just started working with Britney on her wedding dress, and it soon progressed into my first covert operation. Britney was being followed everywhere by paparazzi, who were eager for news on the marriage. Monique suggested we hold the fittings in my office because no one would expect to find Britney there.

When Britney, along with her mother and the rest of her entourage, arrived at my office, they were being followed by paparazzi. I was waiting in the garage of the house and popped the garage door open so they could drive right in. The front of the house was all closed up, so no one could see where they went.

Britney walked into a room of wedding gowns and immediately went to one dress, a simple strapless ivory gown. We thought we had months to put this gown together, but her wedding planner Alison Fox called and asked whether Monique could finish the dress in two weeks, even though the wedding was scheduled for much later. I could tell something was up, but we finished the gown in time, and I delivered it to Alison's office and left town on a little holiday. Soon I was getting phone calls from reporters who said that Britney Spears had gotten married in Monique's gown. I had to act fast to make sure my client got credit. Once I confirmed that the wedding had occurred far ahead of schedule and that Britney had worn Monique's dress, I sent out a press release that gave all the details about the gown.

I still can't believe the wildfire of press Monique received, particularly in the celebrity weeklies. This one wedding took Monique's career to a whole new level. Britney was at the pinnacle of her career, and she'd pulled off a surprise wedding—the press couldn't get enough. A month later,

Newsweek, which rarely does any kind of fashion writing, did a feature on Monique. Britney had done her job, and thanks to some fast thinking and worldwide reporting, my client walked into the spotlight overnight.

THE INTERNET TRAIN
IS LEAVING *the* STATION

Attention spans are shrinking rapidly in today's world, so the need to diversify and get noticed through over-the-top extremes, as Lady Gaga has done, is not surprising. Celebrities are now looking for new ways to collaborate with the media and keep interest in their names alive. One of the most promising areas for promotion in the world of fashion and accessories is the ever-expanding Internet.

One day I got a phone call from Gene Simmons, the bassist in the band KISS. Of course, I thought someone was pulling a joke on me until he said, "I'm the guy with the tongue"— it was then that I recognized his voice. He wanted to talk about launching his clothing line, and though it wasn't the right product for me at the time, I told him how smart he had been for building his brand through numerous commercial avenues—all independent of the band. Gene is an example of a celebrity who has used his fame as a launch pad for business success (this built-in media interest makes him exactly the type of individual who can really help out a brand). That day on the phone, he said something I'll never forget: "If the train is leaving the station, I might as well fill the seats."

Today, the Internet train is leaving the station, and we all have to fill the seats. The Internet opened doors for all of us looking to promote product. We are now no longer limited to pitching to just newspaper and magazine editors—we have a vast, varied, and powerful network that can reach almost any corner of the globe.

In those early years, before the Internet really caught on, magazines imposed a rule on themselves: They would keep advertisers and editorial separate. However, this "separation of church and state" crumbled when the economy took a dive and advertisers began wondering if their ads really sold merchandise. They realized that even if they advertised in a magazine, there was no guarantee they'd get any kind of mention in the non-advertisement pages. Giorgio Armani began asking why, as an advertiser, his products weren't also used in editorial articles. By pulling his advertisements briefly, he single-handedly changed how magazines selected editorial products.

This change ended up bumping out some of the newcomers and smaller players; now, magazines were obliged to write about and promote the companies that advertised in their pages before they gave anyone else a chance. In this new landscape, if your business didn't have the funds to advertise (and sometimes, even if it did), we looked to the Internet—our version of the Wild West—because bloggers and website curators needed content that we could help create.

> *"The power of the Internet is so huge. Information on what celebrities are wearing is related worldwide in a minute."* —FASHION DESIGNER HERVÉ L. LEROUX

In 2005 when Sean Combs first launched his fragrance, Unforgiveable for Men, he started by posting videos on YouTube. This created buzz and began building a customer base for his fragrance. Then, in 2007, when he introduced the women's fragrance Unforgiveable for Women, he took it up a notch by having the launch party broadcast live on MySpace.

In 2008, Procter & Gamble hired Taylor Swift to launch the Venus Embrace Razor, and the singer blogged on her website, sharing thoughts on the product along with her summer vacation and tour. Showing consumers that Taylor had integrated the product into her life was far more effective than simply showing her face in a traditional TV or print ad.

These types of big, corporate Web promotions are commonplace now, but I like to look at these ideas and figure out how they can work for

Photo Courtesy of Jay Godfrey

Designer Jay Godfrey.

my clients. One client, dress designer Jay Godfrey, hesitated to loan his dresses out to reality stars. He thought these girls weren't the right demographic for his brand, but the savvy businessman soon figured out they had a big following—particularly online—and could help promote his line. The result was a direct impact on sales numbers whenever reality royalty were seen in his products or talked about them online. Jay figured out firsthand why so many companies that have contracts with reality stars are demanding a certain number of favorable tweets in the celebrity's contract. (Now you know why some stars tweet so much!)

> *"I see a direct impact in sales when Lauren Conrad and Kim Kardashian wear my dresses. These stars are talking about what they are wearing on their shows, on Facebook and Twitter, and on their own websites. This always helps!"* —**DESIGNER JAY GODFREY**

INFLUENCERS *on the* WEB

Website giant eBay recently launched a new fashion destination, Fashion .eBay.com, and tapped some top celebrity stylists as brand ambassadors. These stylists are busy tweeting, recommending bargains, and hosting their own videos about shopping. eBay now promotes, on average, more than nineteen million daily listings based on the latest trends, and its ambassadors are bound to sell more than a few items. eBay now boasts an annual worldwide $5.45-billion apparel business. Keep in mind that your own set of brand ambassadors can help influence and connect you to buyers eager to find new merchandise. It's not always celebrities who sway a customer; as in this case, it's the celebrity stylists who can turn a celeb on to your goods.

There are websites and blogs for any product imaginable. An increasing number of bloggers are focusing their sites on niche products, and social media platforms like Facebook and Twitter have been critical tools in quickly building a following that is interested in these niches. For example, there are countless shoe websites, including some fun ones with names like Shoebunny, Lucky Toes, Pugly Feet, and Hemlines and Heels. Jaime Palmucci launched DenimDebutante.com in June of 2010 as a way to indulge her passion for denim and provide visitors with her unique point of view. "A lot of denim websites focus on price point and style," said Jaime, "and I wanted to focus on fit as well." DenimDebutante.com has garnered more than 300,000 unique hits and has thousands of followers on Twitter. If you are a denim brand, these numbers are definitely worth making note of.

As you think about working with bloggers to promote your products, go with your instincts and never discount the promising newbie. Tavi Gevinson started her "Style Rookie" blog in 2008 at age eleven. Her audience grew rapidly, and she was the subject of a *New York Times Magazine* story. According to *The New Yorker*, she has had as many as 50,000 daily readers, and she is now a frequent guest at fashion shows.

NEW MEDIA *for* NEW TIMES

I am so excited about the world of social media and how it is changing the way consumers shop. There is a whole generation that shops via the Internet. Mash up the relationships you build with a few celebrities, and then let them help build awareness and momentum for your business through the content they distribute to their fans.

Social media has been a great boulevard for celebrities to stay in front of their fans. A *BusinessWeek* article ("Build a Marketing Platform Like a Celebrity," August 15, 2009) quoted MC Hammer—rapper, dancer, preacher, and star of A&E's *Hammertime*—as saying, "The distance and relationship between the creator of content and consumer has shortened." Hammer connects with his fans via his blog and Twitter feed. "My followers have a better understanding of my brand as a result of social media," Hammer said. "The need for both quality and quantity allows for more brand awareness, which ultimately increases the quality and quantity of your followers." Collaborating with a celebrity who, like Hammer, clearly understands social media can help you tell the story of your brand—as long as your demographic responds to your social media–savvy star. Once you realize that celebrities are looking for exposure and media opportunities, it should make it easier for you to engage them, especially if they are a good fit for your business.

Sobe Lifewater looked to influential artists to design products like board shorts, T-shirts, and hats, which it gave away over one summer. The trick was that consumers had to follow the program on Twitter to learn where to get the freebies. When Fallout Boy's Pete Wentz tweeted about it to his two million followers, sales jumped 52 percent. "You know, you can't buy this kind of media," said Jill Beraud, chief marketing officer and president of joint ventures for PepsiCo Beverages Americas, in *Women's Wear Daily* (November 3, 2010). "Not a dime was spent on public relations."

In the digital world, more is more, and most of your efforts will scale up at a very low cost. The more eyes that see your message, the more people pass that message on—with a simple push of a key, not your cost of a press-run, fax, or phone call.

"People who are famous want real partnerships with companies. They don't want two-year deals or two-and-a-half-year deals . . . They want to play the long game." – BRYAN LOURD, MANAGING PARTNER OF CAA, A TOP TALENT AGENCY, IN *WOMEN'S WEAR DAILY*

Nau, a sustainable and urban outdoor clothing company based in Portland, Oregon, effectively uses social media to communicate with its customers and to carve out its identity in today's fast-paced world. The DNA of the brand is immediately perceived through the website, even though the site's main purpose is to sell clothing. Humility and a personality is seen through photos of the company's friends—titled "The Provocateurs"—all wearing Nau. Actor Adrian Grenier from *Entourage* is pictured wearing a 100-percent recycled polyester blazer.

Adrian's charity of choice gets a well-produced video on the site, with the A-list actor narrating. A sense of community is exchanged in a few words, with *Entourage* and Adrian Grenier fans directed to the site (also through social media) so Nau reaches new customers.

Part of the success of any social media campaign is having bloggers from every market and niche write about what you are doing. Enlisting Adrian's participation encouraged entertainment and charitable blogs to mention Nau's activities, which might not happen without the actor's involvement and testimonial about the brand. Nau takes it a step further by promoting other websites with "like minds," each with a target market that fits Nau's own audience.

GETTING *the* RIGHT SHOTS

In addition to providing new outlets for exposure, the Internet also assists in many of my tasks as a celebrity marketer. Photo websites like WireImage .com, GettyImages.com, and PRPhotos.com were the first to make it easier to find an image of a celebrity wearing a client's product.

> *"The Internet has had a huge impact on the red carpet. It used to be that what celebrities were wearing to events was the domain of Hollywood and New York. Now, because of WireImage and all the celebrity websites, these pictures are everywhere."* —MERLE GINSBERG, AUTHOR, FASHION JOURNALIST, EDITOR-IN-CHIEF OF FASHIONRULES.COM, AND TV SHOW GUEST

If I knew in advance that a celebrity was wearing a client's product on the red carpet, I'd contact photo agencies covering the event to get up-close shots. These are particularly helpful for my jewelry clients, who often wear multimillion-dollar jewels that are hard to spot, especially with long hair extensions. For an extra fee, the photo website will post a credit such as "Earrings by Chopard" or "Dress by Gustavo Cadile." These websites can become your partner, helping you get the word out about your merchandise. Why do it? Because editors all over the world click on these popular sites each morning and pick through photos of the previous evening's events, looking for celebrity images of trendy colors, jewels, hair, makeup, shoes, and handbags. They spot trends started by celebrities and illustrate them with the photos these sites provide. One fashion site, StyleSpot .com, tracks what celebrities are wearing so viewers can copy the styles. To drive retail sales, the site links the red carpet photos to online stores from Neiman Marcus and Barneys.

"Over the course of my networking journey, I was becoming familiar with various press contacts, so I would send them, along with countless others on a huge press list I had built through extensive research, every paparazzi shot that I came upon, along with the story of my brand as a pitch for a potential story. People Magazine *bit, giving us extensive brand awareness, with a brand-appropriate celebrity."* —NANCY GALE, **DESIGNER AND OWNER OF JAMAH HANDBAGS**

Chopard made it easy for editors to use images by providing photos of a celebrity wearing Chopard and purchasing full usage rights from the photo agency. By attaching the photo and letting editors know there wouldn't be any photo-rights issues or costs, Chopard's photos were more likely to be used than those of the competition. Chopard's approach is costly, so for most clients, I'd send a watermarked photo along with my press release and let them know where the photo can be purchased if they used this photograph. These images can also be purchased for your own website. I recommend creating a page on your own website titled "Celebrities" or "VIPs" with photos of the celebrity using, wearing, carrying, or sipping your commodity.

Below are some popular sites that regularly post photos of celebrities wearing the latest fashions. Many of them are scrutinized regularly by celebrity-conscious purchasers, as well as—and not unimportantly—by industry insiders seeking to keep current:

Women's Wear Daily (WWD.com)

Entertainment Tonight Online (ETOnline.com)

E! Online (EOnline.com)

Fashion Rules! (FashionRules.com)

BeautifulStranger.tv

because im addicted (BecauseImAddicted.net)

Coûte Que Coûte (CouteQueCoute.blogspot.com)

YouTube.com

Net-A-Porter.com

Polyvore.com

Signature9.com

Styleite.com

StyleSpot.com

Style Sample Magazine
  (StyleSampleMag.com)
TheGlamourai.com
Vogue Italia (Vogue.it)
My Fashion Database
  (MyFDB.com)

StyleChick.com
TheDailyBeast.com
HuffingtonPost.com
Style.com

You must be very careful when you use photographs. Say a celebrity has been photographed with your product. Before you send this priceless photo off to *People*, you need to get permission from the celebrity and photographer to use the image. Things can get ugly quickly when this basic protocol isn't followed.

One upscale maternity clothing brand had used a photograph of an A-lister on its website without the star's signed permission. The store had given her a healthy gift certificate to shop in one of their stores, and the celebrity was delighted to use it at the Beverly Hills store; she even sent flowers to the staff. But her attitude changed when her management saw her photo on the website.

After a friendly $45-million phone call from the star's attorney, the photo was removed. The point is that celebrities view themselves as brands. A seemingly innocent photo of a famous person holding your product can jeopardize a future paid endorsement from a larger competitor. The Internet is still the new frontier, and while many start-up brands can get away with using certain celebrity images, I would still suggest treading carefully so you don't risk getting a call from a high-powered attorney.

THE SMALL SCREEN
IS GETTING BIGGER

Stacy London, costar of TLC's reality show *What Not To Wear*, recently launched a new business that appeals to regular people looking to hire their own personal stylist. Style for Hire is a service with a network of stylists who have a clear understanding of body types. The company takes a commission from stores, and although the clients are not Hollywood stars, the company's stylists, who are located throughout the country, are just the kind of influencers you need to spread a buzz.

But where did Stacy's buzz come from in the first place? From her appearances on television, of course. In your search for the attention of consumers, don't ignore the fact that the popularity of fashion-oriented reality television shows is at an all-time high. There's *Project Runway*, *America's Next Top Model*, *Stylista*, and the plethora of shows on the Style Network, to name a few. *Elle* magazine's fashion editor, Joe Zee, can be spotted on his Sundance Channel show, *All On the Line*.

And then there are the viewers who tune in to E! Entertainment Television for the entire day of big award ceremonies, watching all of the pre-award shows. In my search for anything new, I've seen stories on teeth whitening, undergarments, watches, hair styling, and favorite lipstick colors. Since they have hours of airtime to fill throughout the entire day of a big award show, entertainment media is a great place to start promoting your product. I frequently negotiated and bartered deals for a designer client to appear on one of the myriad of shows that coo over product in exchange for merchandise giveaways to viewers, TV journalists, and sometimes producers.

Oprah Winfrey—or "Hope-rah," as I call her—is the holy grail of TV celebrity marketing. It's no secret that anything Oprah loves (or endorses) flies off the shelves. The UGG boot, which has been a favorite with the Hollywood set, is a perfect example. Its appearance on *Oprah* as one of her ten favorite holiday gifts sparked a buying frenzy, making the boot a footwear phenomenon. Oprah's Book Club, a feature of her show spotlighting her favorite new books, is recognized for its ability to create bestsellers. Winfrey has even launched the careers of Dr. Oz and "get real" psychiatrist Dr. Phil, both of whom became well known through regular guest appearances on her show, and now endorse products on their respective shows as well.

Talk show host Wendy Williams makes fashion a major conversation piece on *The Wendy Williams Show*. She says of her wardrobe, a mix of pieces from Target and Chanel, "It's always high-low for me. It's got to work for my budget. I think a lot of women feel that way." Her website details each day's on-air outfit head to toe, so why not pitch Wendy with your product? When she goes for it, you've just created another opportunity to advertise because your products were seen on this popular program.

When skateboarder Rob Dyrdek teamed up with Carl's Jr. to reach the hungry eighteen- to twenty-four-year-old male—a demographic they both share—they went beyond the old-fashioned TV commercials that might have characterized the relationship in the past. On YouTube, Rob can be seen skateboarding his way through a Carl's Jr. wearing the brand's signature yellow star and drinking from branded cups. The video received 500,000-plus hits. In return, Carl's Jr. built a skate park in downtown Los Angeles, which Rob featured on his *Fantasy Factory* series on MTV.

When finding television partners—as with all other types of celebrity marketing—it's all about collaboration, partnership, and filling all the seats before the train leaves the station.

MAKING *the* PITCH

I asked the fashion editor at *Us Weekly*, Sasha Charnin, how she likes to be pitched.

Here's what she said:

> Short and sweet. I like e-mails with pictures, JPEGs, PDFs—I'm a fashion person who needs to see pictures, not thumbnails. I also love it when the pitch is to the point. We need the brand and celebrity in the subject line. But most importantly, we need a pitch that has celebrities attached to the item. If the celebrity is photographed in

the item, even better. That just confirms that they have worn it or used it or even loved it. But that's the chief directive for the magazine. If there are no celebs, it has to wait . . .

If you send something to Sasha and she doesn't bite the first time, she nevertheless saves your information: "I usually drag all blasts and files onto [my] desktop and file [them], so I always have a [record]."

If you're wondering if your backyard brand can stand up and make the pages of *Us Weekly*, Sasha adds:

> If a mom-and-pop designer or label has a few celebrities connected to the brand, you have the building blocks to celebrity marketing. We usually find this in personalized jewelry companies, T-shirt companies . . . smaller start-up designers who don't have advertising budgets or huge backing. If they have a celebrity mom who ordered some pendants with their kids' names on it . . . maybe have a testimonial from that celebrity . . . that's a good start.

While you're working to get your favorite star to visit your store, you should be busy building a database of key contacts. This includes influential journalists, bloggers, customers, potential clients, and websites and social networks where you'll want to share information about the visit and post a photo. Leveraging the Internet is an absolute must for brand building.

Since it might take a while before you have celebrity marketing nailed down, try targeting local VIPs like sport stars (the tennis pro or the winning basketball coach) or a TV journalist, politician, or admired leader of a neighborhood charity. They can help spread the word through local media. Consider hiring a professional photographer, or at least make sure you take photos to document the event.

Lots of publications have tight budgets to work around and might be interested in featuring your event, but might not have the money to send their own crews and photographers. In this situation, follow Chopard's lead and make it as easy as possible for a publication to get the images. Offering your own photographs could guarantee coverage in your local newspaper or magazine.

Orlando Bloom once said, "I know you can be up one minute and dropped the next, so I'm trying to maintain a steady course so I can have some longevity." Take it from Orlando—when you're trying to get your product into the hottest magazines, TV shows, and websites, slow and steady wins the race, especially when you're starting out. Keep pushing forward consistently as you reach for the stars.

Learning the Landscape

- Thirty percent of U.S. magazines feature celebrities, so make a list of the celebrities that magazines continually feature and approach a celebrity from the list.

- Build an ongoing media database. The Internet is your best friend when it comes to distributing content quickly and connecting with customers who are one click away from a sale.

- Don't just tell your story to the media—show your story. Whether professional or self-taken, photographs are essential.

- Always make sure you understand any photo rights before using someone else's photo.

CHAPTER 6

WHAT *Can* GO WRONG

"Celebrities make so much money! Why can't they buy their own clothing?"

I hear this question from potential clients and the general public over and over again. Why do designers lend or give product to celebrities free of charge? The biggest reason is if the right celebrity is seen wearing something and the press picks up on it, the result is hundreds, thousands, or even millions of dollars in publicity. In essence, this is free advertising; the cost is nothing compared to the amount of exposure. But the downside is that sometimes you have to take risks, especially when you're dealing with a capricious celebrity or stylist or an extremely valuable item.

And I know this from experience: The bigger the star, the more chances for things to go wrong. Sounds pretty negative, right? Then why bother aiming high with celebrity marketing in the first place? The answer is that the payoff when things go right is huge. However, you should plan for the worst and be prepared for any surprises that might await you on your way to that big payoff.

Imagine uber-couture designer Elie Saab's frustration when he shipped a gown from Paris to Phillip Bloch in Hollywood, only to have it not be used; in addition to the disappointment, a shipment from Paris is very costly and includes customs taxes added on to an already hefty fee. Yet, read the rest of Phillip's story for the Hollywood happy ending. Bloch recalls:

> Elie Saab was a completely unknown designer from Lebanon when I saw the dress early in 2001. A client of mine, Annabella Sciorra, was nominated for an Emmy for Best Supporting Actress in a Drama Series for her role in *The Sopranos*. Everyone thought Annabella would win—especially me—and the dress was perfect for her. Five days before the ceremony, Annabella called me and said, "That's a winner's dress, and I'm not going to win." She was convinced the dress would be too much for a nominee who wouldn't win. Well, unfortunately, Annabella's intuition was correct. I often say, in fashion history the right dress finds the right person at the right time, so Elie Saab's burgundy embroidered sheer illusion gown was destined to be on the rack until a winner was ready to wear it.

It just goes to show that even the best stylist can't always predict the winner. Fortunately, Elie's burgundy dress didn't go to waste. Phillip continues:

> When Halle Berry got her Academy Award nomination for *Monster's Ball*, I knew I had the right dress, and no one had worn it yet. It was interesting to me that Elie's collections always got attention, but nothing over the top. After Halle's Oscar win and all the attention that dress got, Elie's front row at his fashion show was lined with representatives from every magazine, including "the" André Leon Talley from *Vogue*. That moment in time made Halle Oscar royalty and a fashion favorite. It even helped boost me higher in the ranks of celebrity stylists and made me a fashionista extraordinaire. I was still riding high on the wave when I dressed eleven celebrities for the Oscars, but that Halle moment was the tidal wave. Elie's career just keeps getting stronger and stronger. Halle's acceptance was always labeled as over a million dollars of free press in one exciting moment.

Halle Berry in Elie Saab's dress on
the night of her Oscar win.

AP Photo/Laura Rauch

Sure, this story ends well, but Elie had to endure the frustration of the dress not being used the first time around—and, had Halle not won, Elie's dress wouldn't have gotten nearly the amount of attention it did. I've had countless clients send product to a celebrity without glowing results, and for every success story like this one, I have hundreds of efforts that didn't boost success. It's a challenge to work in this niche, and there's a lot that can go wrong, but if you're prepared for the potential pitfalls, you'll be much better off.

Thinking big picture and following my motto of persistence and adaptability are the best ways to make celebrity marketing work out for you; otherwise, the ups and downs that are a part of this business can easily make you disappointed and bitter.

KEEPING *the* FAITH

Another Lebanese fashion designer, Georges Chakra, took a road to working with celebrities that was certainly a rockier one than Elie's. On his first attempt to dress an international star, I introduced the idea of designing a custom gown for the formidable actress Helen Mirren when she was nominated for an Academy Award for *The Queen*. Georges was up to the challenge, and Helen's stylist got the perk of making a trip to Paris to discuss ideas with him. Based on comments from the stylist, Georges made a beautiful red duchess satin gown with crystal-beaded sleeves. The stylist took the gown to Helen's Oscar fitting, along with hundreds of other breathtaking gowns, and Georges's made the final cut. Helen had narrowed down her selection to just a small handful of dresses, and she had them all altered to fit her so she could make her ultimate decision on the day of the Academy Awards.

I called frantically all day and finally heard that Helen had decided to wear Georges's gown. Once I had a confirmation I quickly sent out a press release with the gown's description. Within minutes, I got phone calls from

Photo by PR Photos

Helen Mirren on the Academy Awards
red carpet wearing Georges Chakra.

some of the media to which I had sent the release, asking whether I was 100 percent sure Helen's gown was a Georges Chakra design, since another designer was also claiming the gown was theirs! Most award shows air later in the evening, so I hadn't actually seen Helen in the gown yet. My client and I stayed on the phone all night from different parts of the world until at last I saw Helen walk onstage in Georges's gown. I'm glad we got to enjoy that moment of triumph, but it was terrifying to think that I'd sent out a press release in error. And the next time we tried the same formula for success, we weren't so lucky.

For the 2010 Academy Awards, I dutifully contacted all the nominated actresses and presenters about wearing a Georges Chakra couture gown to the big event. Unfortunately, I was shot down by every single one. The film *Precious* was nominated, and I had confirmed that Mariah Carey would be attending as a cast member. When I spoke with Mariah's stylist, she liked the idea of Georges making a custom couture gown for Mariah, which got me very excited. The stylist wanted something that was simple but still "Mariah," so Georges sketched up a black high-low gown that showed off her legs in the front and featured a draping train in the back. When Mariah saw the sketch, she made a few changes. Now it was up to Georges to produce the gown from his sketch in a few weeks' time.

In the years I've worked in product placement, I've learned that putting all your eggs in one basket (as they say!) rarely works, and even more so in today's competitive market. I thought Georges had gotten very lucky with Helen Mirren, so I suggested he design and put together a few other options for Mariah's final selection. I knew Mariah's stylist would cover her bases and have back-up options for the ultimate decision, but Georges decided not to do it. On the day of the selection, I waited for their call, hoping to confirm that Mariah would be wearing Georges Chakra. Instead, I got a call telling me the gown didn't make the cut because it was different from the sketch. Georges had added large saucer-like sequins along the bottom draping, and the overall effect of the gown was better suited to the jazzy Grammy Awards than the more elegant Academy Awards. It was a no-go this time around, and Georges felt he had been burned by Mariah and her stylist.

Sadly, this type of heartache occurs often in the world of celebrity marketing. For Georges, I knew Mariah's decision felt like a personal reflection on him as a designer, even though it wasn't—that dress just didn't work out that time. I thought Georges should fix the gown for another event, perhaps by cutting off the bottom of the skirt to make it a mini-dress. Unfortunately, Georges chose to close the door. I also suggested to Georges that we circle back and send sketches or photos of his dresses to the stars who turned him down. He may have been turned down this time, I told him, but there might be an opening for him down the road. This didn't happen, either, and I ended up losing Georges as a client. Someone's head had to roll—and I guess this time it was mine.

PREPARE *to* BE SURPRISED

I've been burned many times because a celebrity promised she would wear a certain dress and then showed up in something else. I've learned not to send out a press release until I know it's certain; the so-called Rich and Famous have almost unlimited options. David Meister designed a gown for Lisa Rinna's Golden Globe red carpet appearance and I arranged a photo shoot with *OK!* magazine before the event. Lisa took one look at the photos in *OK!* and suddenly decided she didn't want to wear the gown.

Your product may be precious to you—but be prepared for loss, or for it being gifted unbeknownst to you. An Academy Award–winning actress once hung a gown worth thousands of dollars on a fence in front of her house; fortunately, I got there in time to pick it up before some stranger walked off with it. Swarovski once paid a celebrity big bucks to help the company launch Christmas products in front of the media for a single day. But Swarovski's spokeswoman insisted on wearing her own Chanel jewelry.

Some celebrities can be very greedy, too. It's the job of their handlers to get the most for their client, so expect to be asked if the star can keep anything you've lent to him or her. I could write chapters just telling stories about experienced stylists that have lost gowns in mysterious ways, through theft, customs officials, or bad assistants.

Who is really responsible for something that goes missing? Film Fashion had a lengthy loan agreement form that stylists would sign, accepting responsibility for anything borrowed from our offices. Yet, when something went missing, typically they couldn't or wouldn't absorb the cost. Costume designers have a guild, which takes these responsibilities very seriously. Costume designers who frequently lose product would likely be kicked out and have a hard time finding work. Stylists, on the other hand, do not have a similar organization, and there's no recourse if you lose something with them. They're loose cannons, and you just have to hope that the stylist you lent product to is a responsible person.

Even contracts worth a lot of money can be easily breached in the world of celebrity marketing. Paris Hilton, known for her long golden locks, seemed like the perfect spokeswoman for HairTech International's line of hair extensions. But when Ms. Hilton spent twenty-three days in jail, missing an important launch party, the brand responded with a breach-of-contract claim, saying she reflected poorly on the brand.

Every celebrity is looking for those lucrative endorsement deals, but not every celebrity has the savoir faire to work in a corporate world. When you find one, consider yourself lucky. Such individuals can avert disaster with even minor displays of knowledge of the brand or company they'll be representing. I convinced my client Swarovski to hire Fergie to wear its red crystal dress in the celebrity-studded Red Dress fashion show put on each February by the heart-disease awareness campaign Heart Truth. Swarovski hires a spokeswoman each year and customizes the dress in advance to make sure the celebrity promotes Swarovski in front of the hundreds of editors covering the event. In this case, Swarovski wasn't

Photo by PR Photos

Fergie representing Swarovski at the Heart
Truth's Red Dress fashion show.

100 percent convinced Fergie was the right person to represent its brand. What persuaded the company that she was? Without any prompting, Fergie suggested to Swarovski's director of PR and marketing that they have a conference call so she understood how to pronounce the company's name ("swore-off-ski") and knew what her role would be for that day. I certainly looked like a hero, and the company went on to hire her for other profitable events it had going on throughout the year.

RING-A-DING

I'll share one more story to warn you of another pitfall that can happen if you are a jewelry brand and want to work with celebrities. Jewelry trends, like chandelier earrings, chunky necklaces, layers of chains, and cocktail rings, have been started by loaning or gifting jewelry to celebrities. It just takes a handful of celebrities wearing a distinctive type of accessory on the red carpet to start a new fashion trend and send buyers to stores. Savvy jewelry brands understand the importance of celebrity product placement to help promote their brand, so it's very alluring to have a celebrity wearing their things.

I've represented a variety of jewelry brands, from Kenneth Cole Jewelry and Me & Ro to the luxury brands Gilan, Harry Winston, and Chopard. There is a vast difference in price amongst these brands, and I knew I needed to take that into account when giving or loaning out items to stylists and stars. Kenneth Cole's jewelry tends to be very affordable, so with the company's permission, I could send their fun jewelry to influential stylists for celebrity clients. The stylists could hang onto the jewelry for their own personal styling kits and use it for photo shoots, and if a celebrity wanted to hang onto something for her own personal use, even better. It helps to have a good relationship with a stylist—that way, if a celebrity takes something, the stylist can let you know so you can watch for the item in upcoming public appearances. It doesn't hurt to have the stylist wearing

Alison Krauss in Stuart Weitzman's million-dollar shoes.

Carrie Underwood in a sumptuous Rafael Cennamo dress.

Designer Gustavo Cadile found a niche by targeting
Latina stars like **Eva Longoria** to wear his dresses.

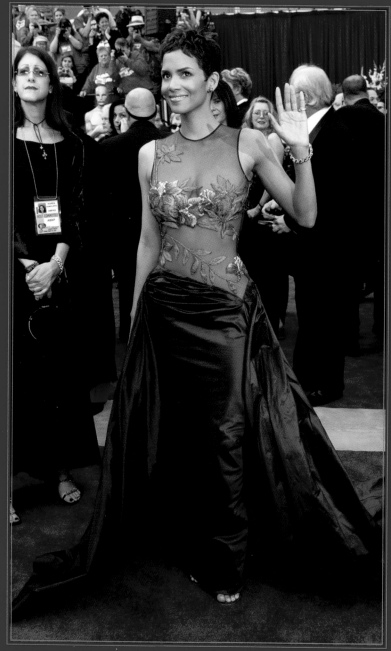

Halle Berry in Elie Saab's dress on
the night of her Oscar win.

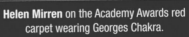

Helen Mirren on the Academy Awards red carpet wearing Georges Chakra.

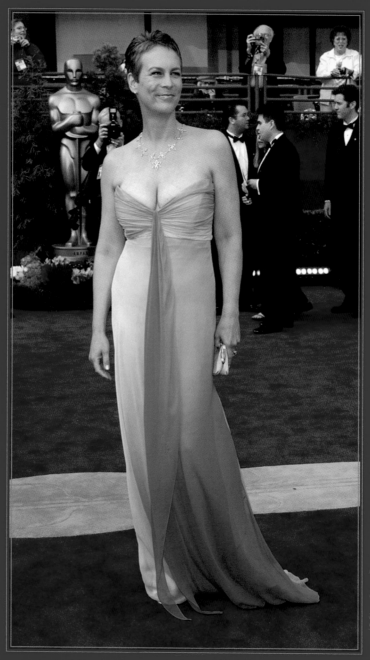

Jamie Lee Curtis in a strapless Monique Lhuillier.

Jennifer Aniston in a vintage Halston
from The Paper Bag Princess.

Designers clamored to dress **Katherine Heigl** in her first big red carpet appearance.

Kim Basinger in Escada after her 1998 Oscar win.

Kim Kardashian, an A-lister in the world of reality TV.

Designer Catherine Malandrino
with her pal **Mary J. Blige**.

All grown up—the **Olsen twins**, fashion designers.

Penelope Cruz, who's often seen wearing Hervé L. Leroux.

Sharon Stone at the Emmys, in the dress
that earned her a case of milk.

Academy Award nominee **Taraji Henson**
looking radiant on the red carpet.

Will Smith photographed
wearing a Worn Free T-shirt.

the product, too. However, not all jewelry companies have the marketing dollars to gift product.

I had the good fortune of seeing some of the most amazing and expensive jewelry in the world, especially during award show season. These luxury brands would fly rare and unusual pieces of jewelry into Los Angeles the week before a big ceremony. At first, I would arrange to show the pieces to stylists or celebrities at a five-star hotel suite or the brand's own retail store, if it had one. Security was a huge issue. Each time an expensive piece of jewelry left the premises, hefty insurance fees and sometimes a bodyguard (usually an ex-cop) would follow. At my suggestion, Harry Winston created a gorgeous "look book" of jewelry we could distribute to the players involved in dressing a celebrity for a big event. (A look book is something fashion companies create each season to show off an entire collection of their products.)

The marketing folks at Harry Winston and I felt that by selecting images from a look book first, the stylists and celebrities could edit down what was realistic for the outfit they were accessorizing. Why risk bringing a whole case of earrings if they're only looking for one or two pairs? This helped for a while, but as the competition to put more and more bling on celebrities grew, stylists ended up holding millions of dollars of jewelry in unsecured places. Rumors of stylists driving off with a bag of jewelry on the roof of their car, home theft, and even someone impersonating a stylist to obtain jewelry followed.

I once worked with a young starlet who borrowed a stunning ring to wear to the Oscar parties one year. She refused to return the ring, and we had photos of her wearing it. I thought the jewelry brand should take the matter to court, believing the little starlet should be disciplined for her dishonesty, but it declined, and the matter went unresolved. Maybe my parents were the only ones who told me that unless you learn the lesson, it will continue to come back. Since that jewelry company didn't press her for the ring back, it was inevitable that she'd pull the same stunt again. It was only a few months later when another client of mine, a young fashion designer who had little money to spend on marketing and celebrities, loaned a dress to this same brat. Well, you guessed it. She held that dress for months and months. My client couldn't show the one-of-a-kind sample to stores that might have bought the dress to sell, so she lost thousands of dollars in potential sales.

RETRIEVING LOANED ITEMS *from* CELEBRITIES

There are honest and decent people in this industry who will be anxious to help you succeed, but remember: If it can go wrong, it will go wrong. Document each and every business deal. I once approached a huge mega-star's publicist about wearing a valuable watch. The publicist said to me, "Don't give him anything of value; he loses everything." I took her advice.

I rarely had to chase down a client's product, but it did happen. In my case, it was up to my client to decide how far to pursue the return of its merchandise with a celeb.

Here are a few suggestions to avoid losing valuable items to celebrities:

- Create a form that clearly shows the items being borrowed or sent to a celebrity—along with the items' value. My form stated that the person signing out the merchandise was responsible.

- If the product isn't returned as promised, take copious notes on that form. Write down the date the items were taken, who you spoke with, and what they said. Sometimes just sending thorough documentation to the responsible party was enough for them to realize I meant business.

- If the value of the product is of extreme value and the person still will not return it, consider reporting the loss to police or filing a small claims report.

- If the value of the product you've sent the celebrity is of small value, let it go and move on.

I've had a few clients who didn't pursue the return of goods (some worth a home mortgage!), stating they didn't want the publicity, which they felt would reflect badly on them. But isn't that like not disciplining your child who has done something irresponsible? When celebrities don't return valuable samples as promised, they usually go on to do it to other people. Despite the fears of the lending brands, public opinion usually applauds penalizing action, and the exposure reflects badly on the celebrity. If anything, the public might question a company working with a flaky celebrity, especially if the actor has pulled similar stunts in the past.

Christmas Vacation actor Randy Quaid and his wife decided to leave a hotel outside of Santa Barbara, California, without paying their bill. The hotel, the San Ysidro Ranch, filed charges. The hotel could have swept the unpaid stay under the rug of its well-appointed lobby, but the hotel stood up for what it believed was owed to it. Just because someone is famous doesn't mean that person should get away with things less famous people would be punished for. There are many perks to being in the spotlight; lying, cheating, and stealing aren't some of them.

Learning the Landscape

- Celebrities are a fickle bunch. Don't celebrate your placement until you've seen it happen with your own eyes.
- What goes wrong at first can go right later down the road. Be prepared for a few ups and downs.
- Make sure to document each loan of an item with descriptions, values, and photographs. That way, if anything goes missing, you have your paperwork in order to help locate the loss.

CHAPTER 7

A MARKETING MECCA
for ANY PRODUCT

I forged new territory and started Film Fashion because I recognized the need for better designer and celebrity relationships. For many years, luxury clothing brands were the core of my business. It wasn't hard to connect clothes with celebrities, especially when I could drop big designer names and offer pricey products.

But as Film Fashion grew, I realized I shouldn't limit myself. I began working with accessories like jewelry, shoes, and handbags. Over time, I expanded and added more casual products like T-shirts, bathing suits, and sunglasses at lower price points. As word about my company grew, I was contacted by companies like Nikon, Shiseido, A Pea in the Pod, Tide, Hasbro, and even the Robert Lighton furniture line. These brands were certainly not the type I was used to working with, but I enjoyed and profited from branching out. As long as I felt I could make something happen, I accepted many different projects and, in the process, discovered that the formula I used for connecting clothing designers with celebrities can work for all different kinds of products and brands. Each new project I took on forced me to be imaginative as I promoted the product.

I truly believe the sky is the limit in today's world of celebrity marketing. This means the opportunities to hitch your product to stars are unlimited, especially since celebrities are looking for avenues other than a film or TV project to help them get exposure. Today, creative partnerships in celebrity marketing can work for a variety of different products.

My husband used to own a beach house in Malibu, which he rented to celebrities. Paul Newman was one of the celebrities who rented it. One day while visiting the house, Paul asked my husband to try a candy bar Paul was introducing for his Newman's Own line. The candy was a combination of chocolate and orange, and my husband thought it was quite tasty. With a wink of those famous blue eyes, Paul said, "Derek, I hawk something every day!"

Let's take a look at some examples of the types of products that have seen success through celebrity marketing.

UNDER COVER

When makeup company Shiseido contacted Film Fashion, it challenged me to figure out how I might be able to help the company. I suggested that we gift the top makeup artists in Hollywood and treat them like VIPs. At magazine photo shoots, celebrities are apt to try something new if recommended by a leading makeup artist, so I helped put together a gift package of cosmetics I knew were staples in every woman's makeup bag, including Shiseido specialties like mascara, moisturizers, and sunscreen. Then, I targeted top makeup artists and sent off the gifts to them.

A number of hair and makeup agencies that represented some of the best in the business, mainly in Los Angeles and New York, were happy to distribute the Shiseido product for me. They couldn't give out personal information, but I knew the product was likely to end up in a celebrity's hands. Fortunately, many makeup artists contacted me directly to thank me. I also followed up with the makeup artists to make sure they got the package and ask whether they liked anything about it. (This type of follow-up is essential, no matter what you are sending out—from mascara to mattresses.)

Sometimes one of the makeup artists would confess that a celebrity loved an item so much, the artist gave away the product Shiseido had gifted him or her. When that happened, I restocked those makeup artists with Shiseido product and then sent the celebrity the Shiseido product the celeb had taken from the makeup artist. How did that translate to press for Shiseido? If you take a peek inside a magazine cover, you can see what cosmetics were used for that eye-catching cover shot; my makeup artist contacts would make sure to credit Shiseido if they could. *InStyle* gave full-page write-ups on how to get a celebrity's look, and Shiseido was frequently featured. In addition, celebrities I had gifted would mention they loved a particular Shiseido product, too—a groundbreaking practice at the time.

A PRODUCT *in* HAND

In the late 1990s, Mary Norton started Moo Roo, a handbag brand, in her Charleston South Carolina kitchen, naming it after the nicknames of her two daughters. Mary instinctively knew she needed a few famous faces carrying her bags to kick off her business. We teamed up and put some of her best samples in the showroom at Film Fashion. The handbags were displayed so that celebrities and stylists visiting the office could pair a handbag with their dress. Charlize Theron, Catherine Zeta-Jones, Halle Berry, and Cameron Diaz were just a handful of the celebrities who carried Moo Roo handbags. Soon, the press started to roll in, and sales followed. "The minute celebrities carry our bags, retailers place orders," Mary said. Her entrepreneurial spirit (along with a little push from me) landed her on

E!'s pre-Oscar marathon. As fans prepared to watch the Academy Awards, Mary talked about handbags the stars might carry that night and got her own VIP treatment as she touted her wares in front of millions of viewers.

Producers of entertainment shows are always looking for something new that might interest their viewers—year round. Mary's Southern charm, colorful product, and a few celebrities who had already used her handbags were the key elements that sealed the deal for her appearance. These shows need content and sometimes hold contest giveaways for their viewers, so they are always on my short list to pitch for clients.

SUN SPOTS

Sunglasses are a staple in Hollywood, the land of sunshine and celebrity. Tom Cruise's movies consistently set trends, starting when the actor sported Ray-Ban Wayfarers in *Risky Business*. Ray-Ban teamed up with Cruise again in *Top Gun*, in which he wore the famous Aviator frames, and the Predator frame had a prominent role in *Men in Black*; it was worn by both Will Smith and Tommy Lee Jones. Big-time corporate manufacturers often pay over $100,000 to have their products in movies, but Michael Schrager, a spokesman for product placement at Columbia TriStar, says Ray-Ban did not pay for placement in *Men In Black*. "It was so perfect a fit and it was so natural," Schrager said. "The look was perfect, the prop master loved it, the director liked it. It just worked all the way around." This is encouraging news for the "little guys," who all need to add prop masters, costume designers, and product placement departments at movie studios to their growing database of potential partners in celebrity marketing.

Oakley sunglasses got their turn in Cruise's *Mission: Impossible II*. The movie opens to Cruise's sunglasses acting as a high-tech video presentation of the mission, which concludes just before the sunglasses self-destruct. After the release of the movie, the company posted a record $100 million in sales—a 39 percent increase—largely due to this appearance. Oakley said it paid nothing to get Cruise to wear its sunglasses. Deutsche Bank analyst Marcia Aaron explains why placements like these have such a strong effect on consumers: "You've got Tom Cruise wearing your product; it's much more realistic to kids than seeing an ad in a magazine."

More recently, Oakley donated thirty-five pairs of sunglasses when the company was approached by a Chilean journalist who was covering the efforts to bring the trapped Chilean miners to the surface. According to AdLand.tv, the snazzy black shades' airtime was estimated to be worth about $41 million in free advertising—all because someone at Oakley was smart *and* caring.

THE COOLEST T-SHIRTS
of ALL TIME

I had been approached by hundreds of T-shirt brands who wanted representation in Hollywood, but I didn't bite until Worn Free came along. What was it about that brand that caught my attention? Well, how about its mission statement:

> Our mission is simple: To recreate the coolest T-shirts of all time. We reproduce rock T-shirts worn by such legends as John Lennon, Joey Ramone, Frank Zappa, Debbie Harry, Elvis Presley, Johnny Ramone, Kurt Cobain, and now Muhammad Ali, to name but a few!

Who doesn't love that? Anyone can be cool if they wear a Worn Free T-shirt. I loved it and knew celebrities would, too. Worn Free already had the actors from *Entourage* wearing the T-shirts, but the brand was looking for some really cool celebrities to help make an impression. With Film Fashion's push, paparazzi shots of Robert Downey Jr., Mischa Barton, Ellen Page, Ed Westwick, Josh Hartnett, and even Cruz Beckham, the son

Photo by Pacific Coast News

Will Smith photographed
wearing a Worn Free T-shirt.

A selection of Worn Free's super-cool T-shirts.

of David and Victoria Beckham, were spotted within a short amount of time wearing the shirts. With those names to drop, pitching the press was easy. The T-shirts' wallet-friendly price helped, too.

Unfortunately, the brand decided not to continue with our marketing campaign. I still love those shirts, but it was unfortunate that Worn Free didn't keep those fresh, famous faces coming up on its website. It's often important to continue with celebrity marketing to keep momentum flowing and keep the company in the front of consumers' minds.

ODDBALL PRODUCTS

It's not only obvious movie-star products (gowns, sunglasses, handbags, etc.) that make a big splash on the red carpet. Let's examine a few head-to-toe examples of celebrities helping kick-start demand for unlikely products.

Once celebrities have made the big time, something they've strived for for a long time, they immediately hide behind a hat and sunglasses. Baseball caps are the obvious go-to for many celebrities. The Von Dutch version, named after a custom car designer and worn by truckers, hit the big time when Justin Timberlake and Ashton Kutcher started wearing the hats. In a short amount of time, Von Dutch hats were selling on eBay for anywhere from $42 to $125. The next trends were fedoras, snug embroidered cloches, and floppy sun hats. A *Women's Wear Daily* article from 2008 reported that many hat makers say business is up 50 percent, and celebrities wearing hats have made converts of men and women who have never worn them before.

This is encouraging news if you are a hat maker, have your own website, and your hats are sold in retail stores. If you can use my tips to get a handful of celebrities wearing your hats, you'll see results before you know it.

Stetson found the perfect partner in Brad Paisley, who always wears a white cowboy hat onstage. His fans know his white hat has to be perfect. The synergy between Paisley and Stetson is a natural one, even if it's a financial deal. According to Paisley:

It's about the image, and it's about the lifestyle and what I want to sing about. It's not like someone's going to mistake me when they turn on *Late Night with Conan O'Brien*, you know what I mean? It's not like, 'Wonder what kind of music he sings.'—*The New Yorker*

"Trends often take their cues from the entertainment world, and the resurgence of hats for men is no exception. Entertainers like Samuel L. Jackson, Justin Timberlake, Johnny Depp, and Brad Pitt have often been spotted sporting brims; hats are worn by the alpha-male characters in the popular cable series Mad Men, *set in the early-to-mid-1960s, pretty much the high-water era of male headgear in America."*
—MICHAEL E. ROSS, MSN LOCAL
EDITION, "PUT A LID ON IT"

Justin Timberlake in a stylish hat.

I never thought a tracksuit would strike gold, but then Juicy Couture's velour version with the word "Juicy" adorning the backside caught on fire thanks to celebrity marketing. Juicy Couture leaped into huge retail sales when the company sent a tracksuit to Madonna with "Madge" strategically embroidered on the seat, and she proudly wore it. Madonna's costumes certainly attract attention, but when she wore her Juicy Couture weekend wear, she lit a flame under the suits. Many middle-aged women lined up to buy the pricey suits, but it was teens who were Juicy's core clientele—a coveted group who use social media to communicate what to buy.

Originally worn by Australian surfers, UGG boots have certainly been around the block a few times. What better way of freshening up an old brand, in this case thirty-three years old, than seeing a few fashion icons wearing the boots and landing on *Oprah*? UGG boots were one of the biggest footwear trends in years, but the brand didn't stop with Oprah. The company introduced its pink and powder-blue versions for the 2003 holidays. Kate Hudson received a pair and was quoted in *In Touch Weekly* saying she loved them. (Even though she was wearing knockoffs in the picture that appeared with the article, the regular consumer didn't know the difference, and the placement still drove demand for UGG boots). "When the shoes hit retail in November, everyone was looking for them," said UGG Australia president Connie Rishwain. "UGG continues to actively court celebrities through direct contact, gift bags, and on-set product seeding," she added.

This is a great example of the importance of continuity and multiple impressions on celebrities and their stylists. These people are bombarded with products, so it's necessary to put yourself in front of them every chance you have. And if you have an oddball product or a new idea, you have an even better chance of catching their attention.

Kate Hudson in knockoff UGG boots.

Photo by Pacific Coast News

MARTINIS AND MAKEUP— *the* MAD MEN WAY

Consider Dean Ogan of Raleigh, North Carolina, who found a creative way to associate a common cocktail with a hot brand. Dean is the owner of Rocky Top Hospitality, and he thought up his own *Mad Men* martini mixer. To help raise money and awareness for Boys to Men Mentoring Network, a nonprofit corporation created to guide boys age thirteen to seventeen on their journey to manhood, Dean combined the Emmy-winning television show with affordable $5 martini specials and door prizes for the best *Mad Men* attire contest. Dean's local newspaper picked up on the idea, proving his cool concept was worthy of some ink.

The Huntington Beach cosmetics company 'Tini Beauty Lounge—which has lines called Nailtini, Liptini, and Eyetini—also found *Mad Men* to be a good fit for its brand. The company motto is "Cocktail Inspired Cosmetics"—and cocktails certainly abound in the show. The 'Tini Beauty Lounge partnered with the series' costume designer, Janie Bryant, to blend up custom colors that users could wear "straight" or "shaken, not stirred."

OLD *Is* NEW

Elizabeth Mason, author of two books on collecting vintage couture clothing and owner of a vintage fashion shop in Beverly Hills called The Paper Bag Princess, shared her ideas on celebrity marketing:

> It's no secret that the average consumer is motivated to consider your brand through celebrity associations and endorsements. The celebrity today is now larger than life, good or bad; they are seen as our modern-day deities. The consumer has been conditioned through ubiquitous advertising campaigns to relate particular brands with the success and lifestyles of the celebrities who endorse them.

Elizabeth clearly understands celebrity marketing, and I was happy to work with her. Elizabeth contacted me about representing The Paper Bag Princess for the Golden Globes back in 2002. Elizabeth had put together about twenty one-of-a-kind vintage dresses she was willing to loan out to the "right" actress. All of these gowns were extremely valuable due to the year of design, the fashion house or designer who made them, or the unique manufacturing skills not seen in today's world of sewing machines. I suggested that Elizabeth put a look book of photos together. There are a variety of ways to create a look book based on your budget, but this is always a good place to start. In Elizabeth's case, we couldn't risk a lot of wear and tear each time an actress wanted to try on a gown, so Elizabeth's photos helped us target her desired celebrities without putting her products at risk. Once the celebrity had reviewed the look book, she would let me know which dress or dresses she might be interested in trying.

> *"I have an expression: 'I don't care if your grandma made the dress.' It's not about the label but about what dress looked the best on the client—whatever accentuated the positive and camouflaged the negative. I never had the fear of using an unknown designer, and actually prefer it on the red carpet."*
> —HOLLYWOOD FASHION STYLIST PHILLIP BLOCH

When golden girl Jennifer Aniston decided to try Elizabeth's original Halston navy jersey dress and then ended up wearing it, our work wasn't done yet. The idea of vintage couture was still relatively new at this time, so we decided we needed to educate the media about the idea of Jennifer wearing an "old" vintage dress, especially since it wasn't just any old dress. The release we sent to the media credited Halston's dress, but also gave information on The Paper Bag Princess. Elizabeth had connected with Jennifer Aniston and was off and running.

Photo by PR Photos

Jennifer Aniston in a vintage Halston
from The Paper Bag Princess.

Elizabeth promoted her unique line of products by taking her own photos of her vintage dresses on a pretty friend versus incurring the expense of a professional photographer, adequate lighting, a model, makeup, and renting a studio. If you decide to create a look book, it can be homemade, or you can hire a professional to help you; the further along you are in your business development, the more important it is to use a professional photographer. It's also important to have consistency in your logo, artwork, fonts, lighting, and sometimes even the model or actor in the photographs. These images can be used over and over to send to editors, use on your own website, or use in other ways you'll find along the way.

One word of caution on the subject of look books, no matter what the product is: Keep it simple, and keep the focus on the product. I had a client who hired a very capable photographer, but unfortunately he photographed her collection with the model sitting on a chair, standing in front of a fireplace, and so forth. The photos were distracting, and although they were fine for my client's use on her own website or for sending out to a celebrity, I couldn't submit them to any media. Because of their extremely tight budgets, magazines, newspapers, and websites often can't afford to hire their own photographers. They rely on you to provide your own product shots with uncluttered backgrounds that clearly show off the merchandise.

UNUSUAL SUSPECTS

Some products and stars might seem at first like strange bedfellows, but many unusual partnerships work. Getting the right chemistry between a product and a Hollywood star can set trends faster than a rocket, and that chemistry can exist with offbeat products, too, not just high-fashion gowns or glitzy jewelry.

Popchips, a snack food maker, recently looked to actor and producer Ashton Kutcher to help create a social-media campaign for the brand. Kutcher was named "president of pop culture," and together they produced viral videos laden with pop culture references. Kutcher also made good use of his Twitter expertise throughout the campaign, and even bought a stake in the company.

Sears and the Kenmore Design Studio picked Thakoon Panichgul to help bring attention to its new line of washer and dryers; advertisements boasted that the hot new designer trusted the machines with his clothing, and he offered his own tips about garment care. This was an odd pairing indeed—most people don't think of fashion designers when they think of Sears. Nevertheless, it was an ingenious way to interest a certain demographic in a mundane household appliance.

Bruce Willis recently inked a deal with Belvédère SA brands to back Polish vodka Sobieski. The company used his no-nonsense image as it crafted a campaign that included "Truth in Vodka" events and lampooned the trendy, faux-sophisticated ads of most high-priced vodka brands.

Remember, the next hot product—and the perfect star to use it or pitch it—is already out there, it just hasn't been discovered yet.

Learning the Landscape

- Hollywood is like the Wild West—there is product placement going on from A to Z, from Accessories to vacation trips to Zanzibar. Even if you have a product that doesn't seem like something a celebrity would use or endorse, celebrity marketing can work for you.

- Remember that the Hollywood touch can freshen up the image of even old or declining products. It can also increase demand for common products that no one might expect to take off (think track suits and cowboy hats).

- The perfect celebrity for your brand might not be interested in your business, or you might not be interested in a celebrity that will approach you. Move on. There are plenty of stars in the sea of Hollywood.

CHAPTER 8

PREPARING *for* HOLLYWOOD PROMOTION

This is one of the most important chapters you'll read in this book. I've worked with very talented designers who dressed some of the world's most beautiful women and enjoyed millions of dollars of free publicity, but who couldn't crack the retail business that would turn them into the next Calvin Klein. Why? Because they just weren't prepared for the impact successful celebrity marketing would have on their business.

> *"Every business must have a foothold in the market in which its product is being distributed. If a business is promoting itself in Hollywood, it should have a clear place and purpose there."* —TOM JULIAN, FOUNDER OF THE TOM JULIAN GROUP, A BRAND CONSULTANCY, AND STYLE EXPERT FOR OSCAR.COM, THE OFFICIAL WEBSITE FOR THE ACADEMY AWARDS

But let's start with an example of someone who was prepared. One of my biggest pleasures is discovering an unknown fashion designer and then layering some celebrity marketing into the mix to get visibility and open doors for the designer. I had the honor of working with great talents like Hervé L. Leroux (better known as Herve Leger) and Alber Elbaz of Lanvin early in their careers. They were unknown in the United States. Paris is a fashion capital, and I believed these two Frenchmen had all the elements necessary to propel them to worldwide fame. I added a handful of internationally known celebrities wearing their goods to their résumés, and U.S. stores came clamoring to carry their collections. Both took that next step slowly to make sure their timing and finances were in order before they made the commitment to marketing by celebrity placement. They made sure they had retail partners and distribution arrangements in place *before* they landed any big celebrity placements, and they also knew they could expand and increase production if demand warranted it.

> *"I want the line to be successful on its own merit. I would love for it to be successful without my celebrity playing into it. But it would be a waste not to use it, as gross as that sounds. I wear it every day, and I'm wearing it during every show of my tour."* —ADAM LEVINE OF MAROON 5, ON HIS FASHION LINE, 222, IN *WOMEN'S WEAR DAILY*

Ina Soltani, one of my fashion designer discoveries, is originally from Bosnia, and she escaped her native homeland when war broke out there. Ina had learned as a young child the intricacies of ruching (a gathering of fabric) and could cut and sew a dress in twenty-four hours. Ina's ideas and inspirations are original, not something she reinterprets from others. I agreed to represent her because of her unique talent, but was worried because her collection was not in any stores. I could land all the fantastic placements in the world, but they would be useless if Ina's wares were not available to consumers. She did have a website and was ready to increase production to meet demand from the work I was doing, but I took on the personal goal of finding Ina a sales showroom where she could make personal connections with retailers across the country. For me, this was one of the final ladders necessary for Ina's business. I hooked up Ina with a sales showroom in New York to close that last step, and then the rest would be up to Ina. I'm still watching Ina's business grow, knowing she has the basics to make the most of celebrity marketing.

BUSINESS *Is* MORE IMPORTANT *than* GLAMOUR

In the early days of one A-list actress's busy career, I initiated an introduction between the emerging star and one of my designer clients. The Emmy Awards and Golden Globes were the star's first big red carpet appearances, and she was being hotly pursued by many designers. We could have taken our chances and thrown my client's gowns into the mix of hundreds of others for her to try, but our approach was to barter with the celebrity by letting her keep those beautiful gowns, plus a generous gift certificate that would allow her to walk into any of my client's stores and select whatever she wanted. She chose our gown, used the gift certificate, and ended up wearing some of these dresses she bought to other photographed events.

The plan worked the first time, but when I learned she was presenting at the next year's Oscars, my designer client decided it was time to ante up with a financial arrangement. This designer is a large international company, and the offer came from its marketing budget; the company reasoned that the value of the international press it expected to receive from her wearing the designer's gown was worth the investment. Still, the designer had to jump through many hoops this time around; it sent her multiple sketches and made four gowns for her to try with no guarantee. The deal was that she would try the dresses just days before the big event and receive payment if she decided to wear one. I'm pretty sure my client's financial inducement helped sway her decision, along with a selection of stunning gowns to pick from.

But when the press frenzy hit and everyone wanted to know all about her gown, the designer's public relations office didn't offer many details, including the price or where the dress was available. This was a significant misstep, and it shows that even big corporations can make marketing mistakes and be caught unprepared when public attention turns to them in the wake of a celebrity endorsement. One could argue that the fashion company got its money's worth in aspirational brand awareness—in other words, recognition from consumers who admire but are unable to afford the product—but if you're in the business of selling clothing and your customers don't know where to buy your merchandise or how much it costs, you have wasted an opportunity.

When Bellini, a baby furniture company, hired us to focus on Hollywood moms and fantasy baby nurseries to build awareness for its brand, the company ran into a similar problem as a result of its lack of preparation. I believed the celebrity weeklies would love showing off star-style nurseries; it was a fresh idea and something I hadn't tackled before. Bellini's idea was to offer some free furniture, and in exchange, the Hollywood mom would agree to let us pitch photographs of her baby's room for publication. Anything that was over and above Bellini's gift the star could purchase at a healthy discount.

Sarah Jessica Parker had purchased a Bellini crib for her baby, but when I approached her about getting it for free in exchange for allowing a celebrity weekly to photograph her nursery, she said no way. I realized we might have set our sights too high, so I looked for celebrities who might consider this kind of tradeoff. Holly Robinson Peete was one of our first moms to agree. She had just moved to a new home and was eager to show off her decorating skills. Before the process started, I asked a few magazine editors if they were interested in publishing a photo of Holly's new nursery.

Once there was interest, the process happened quickly. When the photo hit newsstands and the halo effect of a celebrity loosely endorsing Bellini registered, the problem surfaced: Bellini's stores are all independently owned by franchisees, and not all Bellini stores carried the same goods, making it hard to fulfill orders.

> *"When Mrs. Obama released her official portrait wearing a Kors dress, we had no idea that it was in the running, and I found out from a journalist who wanted a confirmation that it was in fact Kors. Within a matter of minutes, I was besieged with calls and e-mails, so much that my Blackberry crashed."* —BILLY DALEY, WORLDWIDE DIRECTOR OF MEDIA AND SPECIAL EVENTS / U.S. COMMUNICATIONS DIRECTOR, BOTTEGA VENETA (FORMERLY OF MICHAEL KORS)

As you see, it takes more than talent to be successful. Seeing a star using your product is great, but if you aren't ready for the attention and sales that will come from the hoops you jumped through, your effort might not be worthwhile.

Take for another example one young designer I worked with. She sure seemed like a good candidate for success in the fashion business. She designed many dresses for one A-list star, and because both were new to their respective careers, they even struck up a casual friendship. This designer did these wonderful, quirky gowns. There was this strapless leather gown with a big slit up the front that I particularly liked. When you walked, the flaps opened to show a beautiful embroidered goldfish on the lining.

She decided to dress celebrities to make a name for herself, and within a short amount of time, a lot of stars wanted to wear her dresses and gowns. Her A-lister friend became a fan and wore a black high-collar cutout gown that only a tall, thin former model could get away with. When her limo pulled up at the red carpet, Steven Cojocaru, who was doing commentary for *Entertainment Tonight,* got down on his knees and said, "Oh my God. You are a goddess."

This designer's recognition took off, but sadly, her business did not. The back end of her business just wasn't pulled together. She shipped late to stores and didn't aggressively line up retail stores to carry her products; only a small handful purchased her ultra-expensive fabrics. It was a sad day for me when her business closed its doors.

> *"Dressing celebrities is certainly one part of our*
> *marketing strategy, but it's not enough. You have to*
> *have the ability to respond in a very accurate way to the*
> *demands and needs that this exposure brings."*
> —INTERNATIONAL FASHION
> DESIGNER GEORGES CHAKRA

When Jessica Alba strutted the red carpet at the People's Choice Awards, showing off her Burberry knotted platform sandals, retail website StyleSpot.com reported that the sandals generated many click-throughs to retail vendors, but there was one dilemma: The shoes weren't available in stores for another month. StyleSpot.com shows off images of celebs from red carpet events, and with one easy click to a vendor, visitors can purchase whatever they lust for. The website estimates around ten million unique visitors a month—ten million reasons why you need to make sure your merchandise is ready, set . . . purchase if it's going to appear on the site!

Designer Thakoon Panichgul got the timing right when Sienna Miller wore his spring bustier jumper to the premiere of the fashion documentary *The September Issue.* Every store that bought the piece sold out, said a spokeswoman for the designer. "I went to business school because my mom wanted me to take a scholarship," said Thakoon. "I didn't want to do business, but I was good at it." Thakoon's business background gave

Sienna Miller at *The September Issue* premiere,
in a bustier jumper by Thakoon Panichgul.

him the knowledge to hire a sales staff even before pattern-makers and seamstresses when he started his business. He may have made a name for himself dressing Michelle Obama and Sienna Miller, but he laid the foundation that enabled him to stick around long before those famous faces wore his clothing.

Celebrities have tremendous influence over trends and fads in the market and influence consumer purchasing decisions. Marshal Cohen, chief industry analyst with the NPD Group, said, "One photograph of a celebrity wearing a company's product is better than an ad. It's lightning in a bottle." His words are no exaggeration. The celebrity media business has boomed as glossy weeklies devoted to covering celebrities' lives have taken over every newsstand. Celebrity glossy circulation is valued at $1.3 billion a year, and celebrity media TV has over 100 million viewers a week. Those numbers drive consumer sales, so if you're going to harness the power of celebrity media, be ready to deal with the attention, whether that means having enough sales staff or sufficient production and e-commerce capabilities.

"If you wish to take full advantage of the Hollywood publicity machine, it is best to have your brand's infrastructure well prepared to benefit from a celebrity association. Some emerging brands have been known to enjoy skyrocketing sales simply because a young Hollywood It-Girl or -Guy has been captured in the press wearing or using a particular brand, without the company having much preparation. However, it is always best if you are ready for the rise in interest in your product; otherwise you can certainly miss your window of opportunity to capture the market and hold onto it firmly." —ELIZABETH MASON, OWNER OF VINTAGE COUTURE SHOP THE PAPER BAG PRINCESS

BUILD *a* STRONG FOUNDATION

Some companies make the mistake of going after publicity without realizing the costs involved in the publicity itself, or the costs that may be an indirect result of the exposure.

One example of the things you need to consider before you begin marketing to celebrities is the critical investment in a sample collection. Samples are used to show wholesalers, franchisees, or licensing partners the next season's merchandise in a variety of colors, shapes, and sizes. When they view samples, powerful retailers like Neiman Marcus often tell a designer they like the dress, shoes, or handbag but need it made differently or in another color. The designer must then be prepared to pay for the required adjustments.

A sample collection is a huge investment that you may not be able to make once you generate Hollywood interest. I would love to have my own sample line from all of my clients, arranged and displayed to allocate to celebrities for their red carpet appearances. However, I always share one sample collection with the designers' sales departments, runway shows, trunk shows, and magazine requests. It's tempting to fantasize about a designer producing an additional collection for everyone's needs, but this is very costly, and very few of my clients made that investment. However, at least one sample collection is absolutely necessary; it's your business card and the primary way you showcase your skill and craftsmanship as a designer.

Another price tag to be considered when Hollywood comes calling is the cost of flying your product to celebrities and stylists for a trial. Certainly one aspect of my job is acting as a traffic controller. If there is a window in which a sample can be flown to me for a quick fitting, worn to an event, and then returned to the designer, I will coordinate those details. I got to know customs officials and FedEx employees very well! I love when everything falls into place, but with today's stiff competition, it's critical that you weigh these costs and consider what will happen if your product doesn't work out. I'm not suggesting you say no to the celeb who wants to try out your product before saying yes, but you do need to be honest and let the person know if it's out of your budget to deliver the merchandise by 7:00 a.m. the next day. Some celebrities will offer to pick up the shipping costs themselves. They are used to big brands that have a budget to defray these costs, but don't try to keep up with the Joneses. Stay true to yourself and your budget.

Once you have an established business and are aware of the costs you might have to cover, the possibilities for linking your success with a celebrity are only limited by your own imagination and energy. It's important not to jump into the rough waters of celebrity marketing until you can swim. Get your sea legs first by building your business, and *then* consider working with Hollywood stars. Once you're thoroughly prepared, you'll be ready to navigate the fast-changing tides of fashion and celebrity.

> *"Many businesses have been built on celebrity*
> *endorsement. The stamp of celebrity approval has*
> *launched many careers and taken many designers*
> *out of making a few dresses in their spare room*
> *into international recognition overnight."* —BRIAN
> **RENNIE, FORMER CREATIVE DIRECTOR, ESCADA**

FINDING *the* HELP YOU NEED

Whether you are a one-person business or a big company looking to break into this field, you need to decide whether you are going to market your own business or hire someone to do it for you. The question you'll ask yourself is, do you have time to run your business *and* seek out partnerships and relationships with celebrities? At Film Fashion, I worked on behalf of many clients for ten hours a day, and sometimes had even longer days during the busy award show season. The clients I was working for definitely couldn't have handled celebrity marketing on their own.

Some clients would hire Film Fashion to help get things started, and then, as their business grew, they would hire an in-house person to work specifically on publicity and marketing. If you've ever played sports, you know that when you play with someone better than yourself, you tend to play better; well, the same is true here. When a company works with a person who is trained in celebrity marketing and PR, the company will benefit by learning the methods used by professionals who have a track record of success. I've had plenty of big clients with staffs of hundreds who still outsource their celebrity marketing and consulting needs to me.

Partnering up with a PR or marketing firm doesn't necessarily mean hiring the biggest firm in the business. There are plenty of start-up businesses and even one-person companies that might fit the bill for you. A big agency will certainly have the Rolodex to get your business on the fast track to being in front of the right players, but a start-up business might have fresh ideas to help strategize, hustle, and get your business in front of others with similar sensibilities.

You can also come up with a DIY solution, like Kael Robinson did. In 2007, Kael received a gift of a flimsy cotton bracelet with Portuguese lettering on it and instructions to make three wishes while trying it on. She didn't wish to get laid off—but the bracelet inspired her to start her own business. She took a trip to Argentina, where this type of bracelet—the Brazilet—was a hot item. She bought a hundred of the bracelets for $40 from a wholesaler in South America. Since she coached for a girls' lacrosse team, she started her own buzz and PR by offering them to her students for $2.50. "I thought about what would be my target market and how high school is where trends start," she said. "The girls immediately hopped onto it."

Kael Robinson's well-publicized Brazilets.

Her next step was hiring a publicist friend who helped her write and distribute press releases. *CosmoGirl* became the first of several magazines to publish a blurb on her company. The press inspired her to call high-end boutiques: Barneys New York, Fred Segal, and Kitson. She sent each of them a copy of the short article and fifty bracelets in a unique glass bowl that they could display in the store. Now, her bracelets are sold in over five hundred stores worldwide. Kael took the route of marketing her business herself. She started locally by capitalizing on the girls of her lacrosse team, and once she knew her target market—high school—she took the next step and hired some professional help.

Wendy Robbins is another example of someone who has the entrepreneurial character necessary to invent, create, and market her own product. Wendy, author of *Why Marry a Millionaire? Just Be One!*, invented the Tingler, a scalp massager made of bobby pins attached to copper wires, which you move through your hair like fingers. In her book, Wendy tells how she gave away her product at a trade show for celebrity makeup artists. The artists then passed the Tingler on to their dazzling Hollywood clients. "Julia Roberts tingled Catherine Zeta-Jones on the set of *America's Sweethearts*," Wendy said in *More* magazine. The magazine went on to note that after *InStyle* reported on the Tingler, Robbins sold 25,000 in two weeks (she'd sold 3,000 the previous month).

However, not everyone has the time to do his or her own promotion like Kael and Wendy. Nancy Gale of Jamah tried hiring publicists for her brand without success. According to Nancy:

> After going through the PR circuit, I became completely disenchanted. I went through an enormous amount of money and time with absolutely no return. Recognizing that no one can guarantee results, what you pay for in PR is the effort, and this is something that escaped me at every turn. I realized that I could be accountable to the work myself, and the effort seemed worthy of the attempt. I decided that, although I wouldn't hire another firm, I would begin down the path of finding a PR person who would become a part of Jamah on an incentive-, commission-, and possibly even equity-based arrangement.

Photos Courtesy JAMAH

Nancy Gale, owner/designer at JAMAH handbags.

Brad Pitt sporting a JAMAH messenger bag.

Photo by Splash News

Creativity is the mother of invention, and although Nancy's idea isn't new, it was new to her. Nancy's proposal allows her to retain control over her business and frees her up to design her purses, which is what she does best. Meanwhile, her vested partner will be doing what it does best full time—publicizing—but with a stake in the business.

GIFTS *that* KEEP *on* GIVING

Tom Ford, the designer famous for recreating the Gucci brand, recently said, "A muse is getting more expensive." Unless you've had your head in the sand, you're probably aware of advertising campaigns and the millions of dollars spent to buy a celebrity's support. "Pay to play," as it's called, cuts out any guessing about a celebrity aligning him- or herself to your brand and connects your message to the messenger. A few examples include:

- Natalie Portman—face of Parfums Christian Dior
- Isabella Rossellini—Bulgari "Rossellini" handbag
- Brad and Angelina—design jewelry for Asprey
- Reese Witherspoon—Avon

As understandable as it is for these leading actors to ask for big bucks to unite their megawatt name and glamorous faces to a brand, opportunities still exist for people on a smaller budget. Me & Ro doesn't pay Julia Roberts to wear its jewelry—she wears it because she likes it. She liked it enough to wear it in the film *Eat Pray Love*, too.

Catherine Malandrino would wait until the end of a selling season, archive anything she felt was outstanding from that season's collection, and then gift the rest to people who stood out in support of her brand. I always liked Catherine's clever gifting policy because her samples would otherwise go to sample sales at deep discounts. For her, gifting was her way of thanking those who helped her along the way.

*"Rather than gifting to entice, I decided I would
gift as a thank-you. This made it feel much more
real and honest. It helped in discerning where and
with whom I should apply the effort and who fit the
brand in the best way. I do make exceptions, where
the relationship warrants it, but in every case, I make
the decision from a very thoughtful place."* —NANCY
GALE, DESIGNER AND OWNER OF JAMAH HANDBAGS

Phillip Bloch came up with his title—"Stylist to the Stars"—and with clients like his, he wasn't exaggerating. When I asked Phillip about the importance of gifting, he had this to say:

> Let's face it, who in Hollywood doesn't like a good gift? There have always been rumors about bribery and payment, but my clients and I never succumb to that temptation. And yes I heard talk of it, but it just wasn't my thing. I never thought it was correct. However, a great thank-you gift is always accepted, but only after someone has actually worn the dress on the red carpet or for a magazine spread and the shot is seen around the world.

> One of my most prestigious photo shoots was Michael Jackson's *Ebony* cover in 2007. It was Michael's first cover in over ten years in America, and little did we know it would be one of his last photo shoots. This historic shoot took place at the Brooklyn Museum, with Matthew Ralston as the photographer. We put him in white Valentino tuxedo tails on the cover. The look was very Michael, but even better than usual. It was crisp, fresh, and elegant. Of course Michael loved the tuxedo and wanted to keep it, and he did. Valentino was more than happy to give it to him.

> We were also shooting a brand new spring/summer 2008 sample from Yohji Yamamoto. It was a long black duster coat, and when

Michael put it on, I realized I'd have to wrestle him to the ground to get it off! Of course I wasn't about to do that. I was sure the designer would give in and give him the coat. Unfortunately, I found out that they needed it for the other magazines. But Michael was not parting with it, and that's the power the King of Pop has. Though the press liaisons were a bit upset, they finally acquiesced, and off he and his bad self went into the night. That moment was a thriller.

Gifting will definitely sweeten your dealings with a celebrity. Sometimes it even pays off to gift someone who is influential enough to put your merchandise into the hands of a celebrity. More from Phillip Bloch:

I have often been flown to Europe first class with a guest as an extra-special thank you from a designer for putting his or her clothes on my best clients. I was always emphatic about asking for something from a designer (for my client) but always offering to buy it at a discounted price, of course. Knowing that most designers were wooed by the glamour of celebs and their clothes, they would always say, "You don't have to buy it." They would say, "I'll just give it to her as a gift"—and oh-so-many times they did.

THE ECONOMICS *of* GIFTING

Let's take a look at the economics of a photo in a magazine of a celebrity wearing the T-shirt you gifted him. You might pay somewhere near $50,000 (depending on the placement and size of the ad) if you were to purchase an advertisement in *People* for your T-shirt. What value would you place on a candid photo of a celebrity in your T-shirt, perhaps accompanied by a mention of the shirt in the magazine text? You'd have to send your celebrity a whole lot of free T-shirts to total up to that $50,000 advertisement. Many of my clients focused their budgets on my efforts to get consistent placement in the weekly tabloids versus paying for an advertising campaign.

> *"It's been going on since the dawn of time—in ancient Rome, even. This is the nature of how humans do business. Call it a bribe, call it a gift, call it anything you want—and I hear a lot of people moaning about how celebrities get such amazing freebies when they are the only ones who can afford these things! It's all about fame, class, and money."* —MERLE GINSBERG, AUTHOR, FASHION JOURNALIST, EDITOR-IN-CHIEF OF FASHIONRULES.COM, AND TV GUEST

Even if that photo doesn't hit it out of the ballpark for your sales, you can still capitalize on the photo by using it on your own website (using caution, of course). Many brands feature these photos and title them "as seen in" and feature the cover of the magazine along with the celebrity photo. If you are lucky—and persistent—you can get a handful of these celebrity photos and keep them consistently coming along. Those celebrities wearing your brand might just be enough to turn an interested browser into a buyer.

Pamella DeVos, president and designer of Pamella Roland, knew the value of gifting her retail buyers, and her willingness to let me place a dress for her directly resulted in sales. Pamella always hosts a fabulous cocktail party for store buyers on her yacht at New York's Chelsea Pier after her spring runway show presentation. She hires top models to mingle amongst her influential guests, dripping in diamonds and wearing clothing from the show. It's a great chance for buyers to look at her clothing up close and feel and touch the luxurious fabrics the brand is known for using.

At one of these soirees, while I cradled a glass of chardonnay, a model walked out wearing a pink scoop-neck gown with light sprinkles of crystals and feathers along the bottom. I was sold—I wanted that gown in

Hollywood, ASAP! Pamella wanted the buyer of Neiman Marcus to look at it first. We stood side by side and viewed the model together. The buyer felt the pricey gown, which cost $8,000, wouldn't result in sales, so she decided to pass on purchasing it for Neiman Marcus. The next morning, the gown was FedExed right to my office and went straight to the hands of Kim Cattrall's stylist. Kim loved the gown and wore it to a red carpet event the next weekend, landing her in the pages of every tabloid weekly.

Kim in Pamella's gown accomplished the mission of turning heads and turning the pages of the glossy magazines. Neiman's buyer called Pamella and bought eight gowns—which quickly sold. Kim Cattrall helped Pamella sell those gowns and directly spurred Neiman Marcus's buy. The cost was minimal—the FedEx bill and wear and tear on the sample. It was Pamella's first stab at developing brand awareness through a star, and for the small cost, the return was priceless.

For over twenty years I made my business out of bartering and loaning my clients' product, but the stakes are rapidly changing. This tried-and-true method continues to work, but as a star's popularity begins to rise, don't be surprised if the celeb jumps ship. You can't blame celebrities if they want to work with bigger brands that can afford to pay them the big bucks or thousands of dollars in merchandise each season. Most celebrities have a very short shelf life, and they need to strike while the iron is hot.

Learning the Landscape

- If you're in the business of selling and your customers don't know where to buy or how much your product costs, you have wasted an opportunity.

- Be prepared to beef up production of your goods to handle a jump in sales if needed.

- Where is your product sold? Have an e-commerce website or at least one store where consumers can purchase it immediately once they see it with a celebrity.

- Expenses can add up—make sure you've added realistic costs plus surprise costs into the equation. Remember, rarely do you get something for nothing, and this adage is especially true in Hollywood.

- Decide whether you have time to run your business *and* tackle celebrity marketing. Experts on celebrity marketing run the gamut from small to corporate—so negotiate.

- Gifting and bartering product is less expensive than paying for an advertisement or endorsement. However, pay-to-play is a time-tested idea. If you have the budget for it, don't be afraid to test the waters.

CHAPTER 9

GETTING YOUR PRODUCT
to a CELEBRITY

This is the fun chapter, where we talk about how to actually put that product you're so proud of in the hands of a star. We'll walk through various options together to decide the best route for you, but first let's go over what you'll need before you start:

1. A list of target celebrities that includes both realistic and ambitious options to choose from

2. A database of media contacts that is substantial and constantly being updated with new connections

3. A concise summary of your product or company for a press release. I've seen clients write up an entire history about their merchandise in press releases, but one brief paragraph is what I recommend. Grab their attention right out of the gate by using this structure for your release:

   • Celebrity name

   • Event information

- Paragraph about your product
  - A description, plus cost and where to purchase it
  - VIPs (even local) or celebrities who have used it
  - Your contact information and website for any questions
- Your logo, to reinforce your brand

Now that you've got those things ready, let's move on to the principles of getting celebrity attention.

USE GREAT PACKAGING *to* CATCH THEIR ATTENTION

I had a great list of celebrity moms from working with A Pea in the Pod and Bellini, so Hooked On Phonics, a company that produces innovative educational DVDs for children, asked me to do a mailing to some pint-sized celebrity kids. It was fun to get all the essentials the company put together for me to send. There were five treasured children's books, including one of my personal favorites, *Where the Wild Things Are*, along with a complete Hooked On Phonics program and elegant baskets to put everything into. I carefully wrapped each parcel in clear cellophane and satin ribbons like it was Christmas. I included a letter from the company printed on its letterhead. I suggested Hooked On Phonics include a self-addressed postcard to make it easy for the celebrity to respond. Some of the celebrities we sent the gift package to did respond, and Hooked On Phonics was happy. The gift encouraged and inspired children to read, a goal any mom can get behind, but I have no doubt that the artistry that went into packaging the gift boosted the campaign's success rate.

Packaging isn't something to be overlooked. Start by thinking about how you can keep the look of your business consistent. Packaging product so that it embodies your brand won't guarantee a celebrity, but it will present your business in a professional manner. When Film Fashion was purchased by mega PR company Rogers & Cowan, my desk was positioned next to the great publicist Alan Nierob. Alan represents some of the biggest stars in the world, including Tom Cruise, Denzel Washington, and Beyoncé. Before I saw it for myself, I wouldn't have believed how much stuff his clients got with every day's mail. This is why branding your product and the package it's delivered in is so important: You want your gift to stand out for the very reason a celebrity wants to stand out amongst his or her peers—to be memorable.

Kenneth Cole has a unique look to all his materials, from his shopping bags, logo, letterhead, and tissue paper, and right on down the list. Everything that comes from his company always looks like newsprint, in black, gray, and white—always. The minute someone opened a box I'd sent from Kenneth Cole, the person knew who it was from.

TAKE AIM *at* YOUR TARGET

You can have a lovely, unique gift that's gorgeously packaged, but it's useless unless you know where to send it. How do you figure out who works with the celebs on your target list? For good reason, their private information is usually very difficult to find, but you must locate a manager, publicist, costume designer, or stylist to get the ball rolling. I suggest starting with a celebrity's publicist first, but realize this person might refer you to the next person on your list. Don't give up! There is always someone on the star's team who is responsible for her image and who will be interested in your gift. Sometimes I've even been referred to a best friend, husband, or boyfriend!

A publicist will want to know what you are asking of the star. Be prepared to keep explanations succinct. Images of your merchandise are always helpful. You won't want to go through the process of sending your product only to find out the celebrity doesn't like it, won't have time to return it, or gave it to someone else. If the publicist is interested and you send your product, you'll need to be patient. The bigger the star, the more difficult it is to get speedy answers. Us normal folks might examine our mail every day, but a star who is working on a film can be shooting for six months straight. A celebrity on a TV show can film for twelve to sixteen hours a day. So, it takes time—sometimes weeks—for them to weed through everything they are sent.

I follow up every two weeks, and sometimes am asked to resend my materials (yet another reason you'll e-mail descriptions and images before sending anything). Be sure to let them know whether you are loaning, gifting, or inviting them to an event right up front. If there is a fee that will be paid to the star in association with your merchandise or a particular event, I suggest you get contact information for the star's agent, too. Depending on the fee and the celebrity, an agent can get 10 to 20 percent for negotiating the terms of the deal, so an agent might even be the first place to start.

Thanks to websites like IMDbPro.com and WhoRepresents.com, you can easily build out your target list and find out who a celebrity's agent, lawyer, manager, or publicist is. These sites charge a fee to join, but your money will be well spent if celebrity marketing will skyrocket attention to your product.

Let's take a closer look at how publicists work, and how they can help you in your celebrity marketing efforts.

PUBLICISTS

The celebrity's personal publicist is always the first place I start.

Here's how Wikipedia describes a publicist:

> A publicist is a person whose job is to generate and manage publicity for a celebrity. Most top-level publicists handle multiple clients. One of the publicist's main functions is to generate press coverage on behalf of clients and to serve as the bridge between clients, their public, and media outlets.

Large public relation firms like Rogers & Cowan, Baker/Winokur/Ryder, ID, Ken Sunshine Consultants, Bragman Nyman Cafarelli, and 42West represent hundreds of celebrities and have offices in both New York and Los Angeles so they can be close to the action of their celebrity clients. You will also come across boutique agencies and a handful of independent publicists working with celebrities.

Don't be surprised if you end up speaking to an assistant publicist—I learned firsthand that those assistants will one day handle their own clients, so building a relationship now can help you later. Chances are the assistant will quickly answer any question you have. The smaller agencies, too, are more hands-on and have time to figure out whether your call will appeal to their client.

Once you've confirmed with a publicist that it is the best place to send your product, the product might sit in the person's office for a few weeks before he or she will forward it to the client. Publicists often wait to send several items together rather than sending each one separately—even big stars complain about postage and messenger bills!

Follow-up is essential. Don't expect these busy folks to let you know when their star client will use your product. It's up to you to follow the celebrity's comings and goings on entertainment websites like WireImage .com or GettyImages.com. These two are the biggest among many other services like PR Photos, Splash News, FilmMagic, World Entertainment News Network, Pacific Coast News, Patrick McMullan Company, and Elevation Photos, all of which you can use to access the latest photos of celebrities at events. If you know in advance that you've snagged a celebrity to wear your product on the red carpet, these are also the photo agencies you'll contact so you will own your own image. Chances are they will be sending a staff photographer to cover the event anyway, and when you call, you can confirm that they have the credentials secured already.

Elizabeth Mason, owner of The Paper Bag Princess, has this to say about working with publicists:

Some publicists can certainly have a conflict of interest when it comes to asking a fashion designer for special handling for their celebrity client, such as borrowing a gown, samples being sent to them by messenger, images by e-mail, or VIP discounts, as well as outright gifting of the garments, shoes, or jewelry. Oftentimes they try to restrict the designer or brand from benefiting from any of the publicity generated by the celebrity wearing their designs or using their product, thus negating all of a company's extended efforts.

Elizabeth might sound a tad jaded, but she learned firsthand how tricky it can be working with a top publicist who represents an uber-celeb like Julia Roberts. Julia once purchased a gown from Elizabeth's store and, unbeknownst to Elizabeth, wore it to the Academy Awards in 2005. I got a frantic call from Elizabeth the day after the Oscars; she needed me to send out a press release to my media contacts right away. We simply stated the details about Julia's dress and where she purchased it.

Within minutes I got a phone call from Julia's publicist, who said to me, "You will never work in this town again!" and told me I had to run all information relating to media and her client through her before we publicized it. Says Elizabeth, "This publicist simply didn't believe that I should get any benefit from the public knowing where Julia's dress came from."

Elizabeth and I both questioned the validity of Julia's publicist's request. I've worked in the business of celebrity marketing for over twenty years, and this was the first time a publicist had exploded in response to me plainly stating the facts. But it was Julia Roberts, so we acquiesced.

Good or bad, publicists will be your most helpful allies. I found them to be extremely direct, but many bent over backwards to help me and their clients. Remember, whether you are loaning or gifting your product, you're helping the celebrity, which benefits both parties.

When I first started working with Jay Godfrey, Eva Mendes was on his target list. There was something about her persona and style that reminded

Eva Mendes in a black dress by Jay Godfrey.

Jay of a modern Sophia Loren. I did a little research and found her publicist. Her publicist confirmed that Eva worked with a stylist and gave me the stylist's contact information. I e-mailed Jay's pictures to her, and Eva decided she wanted to try a few of his dresses. A little luck and loads of persistence on my part brought Eva my way, and we were off and running. This is just one example among many of how a publicist can provide that crucial connection to a celebrity.

STYLISTS

I have worked with hundreds of stylists over the years and can best describe them as a colorful bunch of individuals. They all share a passion for fashion and clothing, of course. Along with publicists, I found working with stylists to be the best avenue of getting my client's product into the hands of celebrities.

Wikipedia's description of a stylist is a follows:

> Wardrobe stylist is the job title of someone who selects the clothing for published editorial features, print or television advertising campaigns, music videos, concert performances, and any public appearances made by celebrities, models, or other public figures. Stylists are often part of a larger creative team assembled by the client, collaborating with the fashion designer, photographer/director, hair stylist, and makeup artist to put together a particular look or theme for the specific project. A wardrobe stylist can also be referred to as a fashion stylist, fashion editor, or celebrity stylist.

Today, schools train eager fashionistas how to be stylists, but there are hundreds of professional stylists who never receive any formal training. One top stylist started her career as an assistant, learning the ropes until she was ready to step out on her own. Most people think of a stylist as a very polished young man or woman straight out of *Vogue*. This particular stylist did not fit the mold.

Her house (where she kept clothing samples worth thousands of dollars) was unkempt and resembled that of a compulsive collector. Her dogs used the floor as their bathroom. But none of these flaws that would normally have derailed a career in Hollywood could stop the scrapper in her from working tirelessly to become a stylist. She also had a photographic memory and could describe details of dresses she had seen months before that would be perfect for an actress with whom she was working. She may not have been the stereotypical stylist, but she went on to style A-list clients famous for their fashion sensibilities.

Phillip Bloch, stylist extraordinaire, is in large part responsible for elevating the role of stylist in Hollywood; super-stylist Rachel Zoe and other well-known stylists working today need to give him a big nod. Here's how Phillip describes his rise to prominence:

> When I started the Hollywood phase of my career as a stylist, there was no such thing as a celebrity stylist. And what that term meant was twofold in my case: I was a stylist who catered to the celebrity and their needs for the red carpet, and I became a bit of a celebrity on the red carpet myself. In my early days of the mid-'90s in Hollywood, the landscape of celebrities began to change. I nicknamed it the New New Hollywood glamour. Jennifer Lopez, Meg Ryan, Sandra Bullock, Jada Pinkett Smith, Fran Drescher, Julianna Margulies, Christine Johnson, Courtney Cox, Cameron Diaz, Jennifer Aniston, Halle Berry, Angela Bassett, Salma Hayek—these were my girls. But let's not forget the gentleman as well: Jim Carrey, Will Smith, John Travolta, Charlie Sheen, Jimmy Smits, and so on.

> I had worked in Europe for almost a decade before I moved to New York, where I worked with models at the beginning of my styling career. And after a couple of years, I made the journey to Hollywood, where my eye for the chic and my taste for elegance was desperately needed, if I do say so myself. I had all my connections with Seventh Avenue fashion and the European houses. At

that time, most celebrities were buying their dresses at Loehmann's or borrowing from a store called Fred Hayman. Occasionally a Bob Mackie would show up somewhere, usually on Cher. But these new actresses needed the new Hollywood glam, and I was going to give it to them.

I knew how to get in contact with Dolce & Gabbana, Donna Karan, Calvin Klein, and Christian Dior, and designers like Giorgio Armani and Versace had started to set up shop as well on the Hollywood frontier. I was the conduit that could connect publicists, celebrities, and fashion houses. And what was not to love? I made publicists' jobs easier by making their clients look glamorous. I was overwhelmed with the fun and glamour of it all, and was making a few coins along the way, so I was a willing participant.

Publicists dealing with the multifaceted task of keeping clients in front of their fans are happy to delegate their clients' dressing needs to stylists like Phillip and his colleagues. You'll find that publicists will often offer up the names and phone numbers of stylists, which will help you build out a database of stylist contacts.

> *"The best way to get to me is to send me a box of designs! Not an e-mail, not a private showing—a box filled with products I can use right away. I love it when I open a box at 9 a.m. and that same night the designer sees their product on TV!"* —ANYA SARRE, HEAD FASHION STYLIST, *ENTERTAINMENT TONIGHT* AND *THE INSIDER*

Another method of getting in front of stylists is to go through their agency. This type of agency represents wardrobe stylists, hair stylists, and makeup artists. A quick Google search will yield some of the bigger agencies. I found stylists' agents incredibly helpful with forwarding along any information I provided.

I also study magazines to pick up on who the hottest stylists are. Whenever I see a celebrity photo I like, I read the small print usually found along the side of the photo. If you do this for a while, you'll become familiar with many stylists' names. Make it a habit as soon as possible!

Fati Parsia is the successful stylist who helped navigate Catherine Zeta-Jones's glam factor when Catherine first arrived in Hollywood. Fati has this to say:

> I educate, elevate, and share great knowledge with my actress clients. Most celebrities aren't born with a keen sense of style; it is acquired. The relationships between designers and celebrities have been established via my introductions.

Stylists *need* fashion merchandise for their busy clients. Anyone can find Chanel, but stylists must dig deeper to find undiscovered product that might put a celebrity client in the fashion media. How do they like to be approached with these fresh ideas? Let's hear from Carrie Underwood's stylist, Trish Townsend:

> Photos [of products] are a nice start. I can tell by the general style or silhouette if I will be interested. However, I like to touch and feel the fabric . . . take a look at the stitching, feel the weight of the jewelry, check the finishing to see if it has the quality I like for my clients. So, if I get a picture of something and I find that interesting, I pursue the designer further by requesting samples.

I enticed Trish to consider a Rafael Cennamo gown for Carrie Underwood. The gown was so huge it took up the entire stage! That gown would have been too cumbersome for anyone to walk in, but I knew it had great drama, and Trish saw that, too. Trish commented:

> The Rafael Cennamo gown Carrie wore to perform "I Told You So" at the 2009 Academy of Country Music Awards received an

Carrie Underwood in a sumptuous Rafael Cennamo dress.

unbelievable amount of press due to the construction of the dress
and the execution of the staging. The dress was made with approximately 120 yards of a deep red silk taffeta and the art department
[of the award show] added an additional fifty yards to create an
extremely voluminous dress that filled the stage. The stadium lighting matched the color of the dress, making the entire room feel like
it was consumed with the gown. I have never seen so much press on
a dress in my career! The gown was displayed in the Country Music
Hall of Fame in Nashville.

Some brands have even found getting next to today's top stylists, instead
of celebrities, to be effective. When eBay launched its new fashion destination, Fashion.eBay.com, it tapped celebrity stylist Annabel Tollman as
its brand ambassador, along with stylists Rebecca Weinberg, Kate Young,
Estee Stanley, and Britt Bardo.

Rachel Zoe, known for her roster of celebrity clients that includes
Nicole Richie, Jennifer Garner, Molly Simms, and Keira Knightley, works
with online shoe retailer Piperlime.com. Says Zoe, "Apparently my picks
sell out in about an hour."

COSTUME DESIGNERS

Another way to get noticed is to contact costume designers, whom
Wikipedia describes this way:

> A costume designer is a person whose responsibility is to design
> costumes for a film or stage production. He or she is considered an
> important part of the production team, working alongside the direc-
> tor, scene and lighting designers, as well as the sound designer . . .
> Costume designers will typically seek to enhance a character's per-
> sonality . . . through the visual design of garments and other means
> of dressing, distorting, and enhancing the body—within the frame-
> work of the director's vision.

Costume designers are a dedicated group of individuals who are purely devoted to making sure an actor's wardrobe is perfect on the set of a production. In fact, costume designers are so valued in the industry, they have their own award category at the Academy Awards and the Emmy Awards, and their own annual Costume Designer Guild Awards. They can single-handedly start trends through their work in film and even television. Some of my personal favorite examples are the landmark styles seen in *American Gigolo, Annie Hall, Saturday Night Fever, Flashdance, The Devil Wears Prada, Sex and the City, Gossip Girl,* and *Mad Men,* to name a few. And the best news? Costume designers have a budget for purchasing any wardrobe used for a project!

There are a myriad of ways to locate a costume designer, but the easiest method is through the Costume Designers Guild, which is made up of some nine hundred members. The guild will charge a fee to send information about your business to all its members, but it will be well worth your while.

Kenneth Cole is approached almost daily by costume designers about loaning or purchasing his product. Since his merchandise is generic and doesn't display his recognizable logo, he figured out a great way of working with them: He offers them his own VIP card and a 30 percent discount for a year. Not only can he claim to be working with some of the best TV shows and films in production, but also sells his accessories and clothing to them.

Arianne Phillips is one of the busiest costume designers in the business. Some of the films she has worked on include Tom Ford's acclaimed directorial debut *A Single Man,* for which she received a BAFTA nomination. She also received an Oscar nomination for her costume design work in *Walk the Line.* Other films she worked on include *3:10 to Yuma* and *Girl, Interrupted,* among others. Besides her demanding film career, she has worked with Madonna for the past fourteen years on everything from four concert tours and numerous album covers to twenty music videos. She began her career in New York City working with Lenny Kravitz and also as a freelance fashion editor.

With her feet in many worlds and with the respect of many of the industry's biggest stars, Arianne is an example of why reaching out to costume designers is essential.

> *"I began by immersing myself in the world of wardrobe stylists, costume designers, and anyone else that had a connection to that world. I contacted every appropriate fashion agency that I could find in my effort to get in front of the brand-appropriate celebrities. I would invite them to see the product, most preferably at my location, which best tells the story of the brand, always making it clear that if more convenient, I would be happy to come to them. Once the stylist or costume designer had helped me get the product in front of the celebrity, I would scan the Internet daily looking for pictures of my 'wish list' celebs and, sure enough, they began to appear. Then, one day, there it was, Brad Pitt carrying Jamah! People bit, giving us extensive brand awareness through a brand-appropriate celebrity."* —NANCY
> **GALE, DESIGNER AND OWNER OF JAMAH HANDBAGS**

Another more direct method of reaching costume designers is to do research on IMDb.com to find the names of the people you want to reach. Then, send information on your brand through snail mail to the studio, care of the show or film and the person's name. Alternatively, you can look them up on Twitter and Facebook.

GIFTING SUITES

Another popular route to consider when you're trying to get your product to a celebrity is the gifting suite and/or gift bags. The usual types of merchandise on parade at a gifting suite are sunglasses, jewelry, makeup, haircare products, tanning booths, massages, and gym memberships.

These have become big business for companies that specialize in doing them, but I don't have a lot of experience with them; I prefer to introduce product directly to celebrities. You won't find your big A-lister caught dead attending a gifting suite, but it is certainly a way to put your product in the hands of some celebrities. Since you can't control what celebrities or celebrity hangers-on go to the suite, you can't handpick which celebrities will get to sample your ware. The organizer's job is to get as many viable celebrities through the doors, and some will be questionable celebs. Gifting suites are perfect venues for publicists to march out their up-and-coming clients, most of whom will love getting freebies.

> *"The notion of gift suites could be souring. As gifting has become more popular and more public, top stars rarely show up anymore. It would be tacky, especially in this economy, for a Tom Cruise– caliber celeb to be photographed carrying a big bag of free loot."* –ASSOCIATED PRESS

SPOTLIGHT *on* SPANX

Sara Blakely and her undergarment company, Spanx, might sound familiar to you now, but Sara's entrepreneurial spirit had a rocky start. Thanks to her persistence in getting her novel idea in the hands of the right people— including her use of many of the tactics presented in this chapter—Sara was able to overcome setbacks to hit it big.

Sara flunked law-school admission tests twice and floundered in a variety of jobs. One night she was trying her hand at stand-up comedy while wearing white pants. At the last moment she cut off the feet of her panty hose so she wouldn't show off any panty lines, and a new business was born. Her friends convinced her she was on the right track, so Sara put the wheels in motion and started her new company. She came up with a cute and sassy tagline—"Don't worry, we've got your butt covered"—knowing the risqué phrase could help seize attention.

Once she was in retail stores, she started at the grass roots level of marketing by asking her friends to help jump-start excitement for her product. "I called all my friends and begged them to make a fuss over the product and buy them up," Sara writes on her website. "Word of mouth and the media are so much more powerful and believable, so that's the route I decided to go."

She also knew a buzz for Spanx was essential, so she sent off a gift basket of Spanx to Oprah Winfrey. Sara added a thoughtful thank-you note to Oprah, thanking *her* for inspiration. "She loved it and made it her product of the year," Sara says. Sara continued filling the seats in her train by targeting women's magazines, business magazines, and morning TV shows. Celebrities like Valerie Bertinelli, Jessica Alba, Jennifer Hudson, Anne Hathaway, Gwen Stefani, and Sarah Jessica Parker lined up to profess their love of Spanx.

Sara had a few things going for her that will work for you, too. She invented something she believed celebrities would want to know about, and she wasn't afraid to pick up the phone and ask people to try her product. Having competitors like HanesBrands, Under Armour, and Wacoal didn't slow Sara's efforts down. Her cost per unit was low enough that she could afford to take the risk and send samples to Oprah and other celebrities. Once they were hooked, they bought. Tyra Banks was even spotted buying forty-five pairs at Bloomingdales!

My business was built on getting product directly into the hands of celebrities, and in some cases that meant building inroads with the groups discussed in this chapter. There is no magic formula for success, but my advice should give you the tools for celebrity-marketing triumph.

Learning the Landscape

- Take extra time to make sure the presentation of product you send out (the wrapping, box, tissue paper, etc.) tells the story of your brand.

- Include a personal note with your contact information, your Web address, and a brief summary of your business.

- Invest in a subscription to a website that offers reliable contact information for celebrities. Check back frequently to make sure your information is updated—celebrities can change stylists or publicists quite quickly.

- Continue building your list of Hollywood connections by researching key costume designers and stylists. These names can put your product in the hands of celebrities.

- Consider participation in a gifting suite, although you should keep in mind that these might be populated mainly by low-grade celebrities.

CHAPTER 10

FINDING *a* CELEBRITY *with the* RIGHT APPEAL

Knowing exactly who buys your product will help you decide on the best celebrities to be associated with your brand. For example, Miley Cyrus, Justin Bieber, Selena Gomez, and Taylor Swift fill the pages of teen magazines and have a young fan base eager to spend money. If you have a product that will appeal to this young audience, you should do everything you can to have one of these teen stars become a walking billboard for your brand.

Most people don't think of reality stars, no matter how popular, as individuals they want to align their brand with. The "Real Housewives" of New Jersey, New York, Washington, Atlanta, and Orange County draw big numbers and big drama, but when invitations were sent for the Duckie Brown fashion show in New York, none of these ladies were on the list. "It's a generous and loose use of the word to call them celebrities," said Daniel Silver, a co-designer for the brand. "I'd be hard-pressed to have someone explain to me why it's meaningful to us to have them pictured at our show."

Yet, one person's trash is another's treasure. Pamella DeVos, designer for Pamella Roland, seated feuding reality costars Bethenny Frankel and LuAnn de Lesseps right next to each other at her fashion show. Their cat-fight, caught on film, brought in big numbers and tabloid magazine fodder and guaranteed airtime for Pamella's show. The fight "didn't bother me whatsoever," said Pamella.

> *"Partnering with 90210 makes perfect sense because*
> *there is a natural synergy between our Bebe brand and*
> *the adventurous energy and sexiness portrayed by the*
> *characters in the show . . . This integrated marketing and*
> *product placement initiative . . . closely aligns with the*
> *aspirational spirit of the show."*
> —MANNY MASHOUF, FOUNDER AND CEO OF BEBE

Twenty-year-old outerwear company Weatherproof brought some unusual brand awareness through a daring partnership and one Times Square billboard advertisement. The company featured an unauthorized photograph of President Obama wearing one of its coats. The Obama ad resulted in an estimated 1.7 billion impressions worldwide, and showed the company that politicians are the new celebrities for that brand. The company quickly sent two hundred similar jackets to other world leaders. In *Women's Wear Daily*, Weatherproof president Freddie Stollmack said of the eye-catching billboard, "More than anything, it confirmed to me that, in this market, you have to trust your gut and your intuition. The old way of doing business isn't working, but there is room for the new." Taking its success up a notch, Weatherproof paired with the progressive news website The Huffington Post for a "Style vs. Substance" survey. Approximately seventeen thousand participants commented on whether they vote for a candidate based on his or her appearance or qualifications.

"It's important to develop strong relationships with celebrities who appeal to the demographic you are hoping to reach. I have been known on occasion to personally choose not to loan a gown to a particular celebrity when I have felt that their image is not in keeping with that of my brand. This can often be a difficult position to be in when dealing with a celebrity's management team, who may try to get you to dress their B-grade celebrity while dangling the carrot of the future chance to work with an A-lister. Hollywood is a dangerous town to say no in, for the truth is, you never know when that person you said no to today will be the one you need in your back pocket the next day." —**ELIZABETH MASON, OWNER OF VINTAGE COUTURE SHOP THE PAPER BAG PRINCESS**

Many of my clients seek out young, younger, and youngest celebrities without much thought about whether these stars connect with their own clients. When Shiseido picked Amanda Seyfried as a spokeswoman for its line of luxury cosmetics, Clé de Peau Beauté, it gave careful consideration to the match. The beauty line was overhauled, so it needed a face with international appeal, and the young starlet had a string of recent movie hits, including *Dear John* and *Mamma Mia*. Yoshiaki Okabe, general manager of the Clé de Peau Beauté division, said, "Amanda's radiance and sophisticated style are the perfect embodiment of Clé de Peau Beauté." But how many twenty-year-olds can relate to a pricey skin care line? Both Amanda and Clé de Peau Beauté have their own strong demographic, but in my opinion the match-up doesn't quite fit. Amanda's age group of twenty-to thirty-year-old fans aren't buying $60 sunscreen. Clé de Peau Beauté's core customers have been out in the working world for a while, can afford expensive skin care products and a new Lexus, and would appreciate an endorsement from a slightly older Hollywood star.

Zooey Deschanel recently became a brand ambassador for beauty line Rimmel's Lash Accelerator. Here's what she had to say to *Women's Wear Daily* about representing Rimmel: "I shop everywhere and I love the fact you can get such great looks at a reasonable price. I want to be associated with products that are accessible for everyone." She could have opted for a more elite partner, but she liked Rimmel's product and the fact that Rimmel is available at stores like Target, CVS, and Walgreens. Rimmel was smart to go after a celeb whose fan base will appreciate the affordable prices of its products.

Tommy Hilfiger examined the scene of pop culture and knew he wanted to be a part of it. His brand was one of the first to use Britney Spears as a model. "She looked like she was the jeans customer, so we used her in our jeans campaign," he said in *Women's Wear Daily*. "Using celebrities would not only build our customer base, but would appeal to their fans as well." Tommy Hilfiger went on to feature stars like Lenny Kravitz, Jewel, Sheryl Crow, David Bowie, and Iman in its clothing advertisements and Beyoncé in its True Star fragrance campaign.

Colorado-based Maxx Sunglasses has a clear vision of who its customer is. The eyewear company decided on a marketing and sponsorship program with the Colorado Rockies, a major league baseball team, and recently found a partner with professional barrel racer Tana Poppino. Tana's personal story of going from corporate marketing executive to full-time rodeo athlete caught the public's attention when a national magazine wrote about Tana's brave journey to fulfilling her dream.

The eyewear company could have decided to go the Hollywood route, but it felt its high-definition polarized lenses with UV protection and lightweight frames aligned with customers attracted to active, outdoor lifestyles. The brand experimented with taking on an image that would appeal to a more rural consumer, and Tana promoted the product through a variety of marketing avenues and public appearances for the company, displaying the company logo, wearing an assortment of sunglasses, and providing links between her website and the company's.

A spokeswoman for the company had this to say about showcasing Tana in the sunglasses: "We believe her highly competitive nature, her friendly personality, and her credibility as a professional athlete make her an excellent representative for our products." While shooting for the stars might be your end goal, keeping things close to home has Maxx Sunglasses confident its hook-up with a few smaller satellites will influence its customers.

FINDING MR. *or* MRS. RIGHT

One year as I scrambled to figure out who would be attending the season's red carpet awards, I was floored to get a call from Jamie Lee Curtis's stylist asking me about a gown she saw in Monique Lhuillier's store window. A strapless blue ombre gown caught Jamie's eye and, knowing she was presenting and walking the Academy Awards red carpet, Jamie thought the designer would be thrilled to offer the gown gratis or discounted in exchange for the exposure. I agreed. Real women look at Jamie's figure and think, "I could wear that, too." She is so approachable, and that's a quality that sells clothing.

Unfortunately, Monique didn't feel Jamie fit her demographic. I was left with the difficult task of explaining this as nicely as possible to Jamie and her stylist. To her credit, Jamie slapped down her credit card and didn't even blink, endearing me to her even more. Jamie got glowing reviews in that gown, proving that a class act crosses any demographic. Women like Jamie stand for the one-two punch called ageless beauty and smarts, and who wouldn't want that demographic buying your product?

> *"Kate Hudson and Drew Barrymore are in a sweet spot—fashionable, and young enough to inspire Internet shoppers, yet not so young that they're attracting teens or college-aged women who don't have a lot of money for clothes."*
> — *THE WALL STREET JOURNAL*, FEBRUARY 4, 2010

AP Photo/Laura Rauch

Jamie Lee Curtis in a strapless Monique Lhuillier.

Sometimes it pays to pursue an unexpected celebrity or niche. For instance, country music artists have a predicable look and thus are hotly shadowed by conventional brands. When Nashville stylist Trish Townsend hooked up with newcomer Carrie Underwood, she decided to shake things up. Says Trish:

> I have worked hard over the years to try and mainstream the look of country artists. Some of the guys use just one element of Western dressing, such as cowboy boots or a Western shirt, to achieve the look. Many of the male artists tend to bookend themselves with a full Western look, including the hat, embroidered shirt, boot-cut jeans, cowboy boots, Western belt, and big buckle. Most of the guys actually come from a Western upbringing. Their audience relates very well to that image. That makes them seem more approachable to their fans. The fans mean more to country artists than to other artists in other genres of music. Country artists get really up close and personal with the fans, even dedicating a week each year to get to know them better.
>
> It is different with female artists in country music, especially since Carrie Underwood hit the scene. From the start, I wanted Carrie to appeal to fans of all genres of music. I never tried to dress her "country" (for example, simple jeans and a T-shirt or tank). We have taken the typical perception of the female country music performer and made it more mainstream, thus opening up the potential for *all* female performers to broaden their fashion and style options. Carrie's looks are layered and complex, colorful, and sexy. The heels are high and the boots come up to the thigh. The gowns are smart and sophisticated. It has been fun watching and participating in the evolution of the look. I have a lot of designers and their reps to thank!

A few years after Herve Leger sold his company (and his name) to BCBG, he started over with a new fashion business called Hervé L. Leroux. His new name literally translates to "Hervé with red hair," which accurately describes the designer. Herve opened a small atelier on the West bank of Paris, and his funds, like those of most start-up companies, were tight. With no money to advertise, Herve decided to hire me to help him put his beautiful dresses on celebrities. We had worked together successfully in the past, so Herve knew what to expect. He had the back end of his business set up and was ready for the push that can come your way with celebrity marketing. His clothing was sold in one store in the United States, but he needed more retail outlets in order to turn the corner from start-up to star-powered commerce.

We decided to approach the most desired and gorgeous celebrities in the world. *Why not start at the top?* we thought, reasoning that we could always adjust our sights as we went along. Herve is an international brand based in France, so the celebrities I targeted for him had to be faces known all over the world. Our celebrity list couldn't be actors only known in the United States.

> *"If you want a stellar image, you need to land A-list celebs. Lots of start-up handbag companies and shoe designers and jewelry designers use low-level celebs to make their names. When we see that, our perception of the product is all about glitz and has little value. It's important to promote your product through the 'right' celebrity"* — MERLE GINSBERG, AUTHOR, FASHION JOURNALIST, EDITOR-IN-CHIEF OF FASHIONRULES.COM, AND TV GUEST

Once we had our wish list of names in place, I started my due diligence to figure out the best way to get photographs of his collection to the right person. The first person to bite was Cate Blanchett's stylist. To complicate

Penelope Cruz, who's often seen
wearing Hervé L. Leroux.

matters, she asked Herve to make a specific dress from his collection in another fabric and color. In my experience, this type of request is almost always a total crapshoot and usually doesn't work out. Herve's company is so small that producing a completely new dress in a matter of days would cost him a significant amount of time and money, something I wanted him to consider seriously. Herve felt it was worth the risk.

As luck would have it, the dress worked out perfectly, and our perfect-fit celebrity landed in the pages of *People*. The gamble paid off, and since Cate is considered an adventurous icon of fashion, I took the image of her wearing his dress as a stamp of approval to show other stylists. Gwyneth Paltrow, Halle Berry, Megan Fox, and Kate Beckinsale soon followed, all wearing Herve's designs.

Even though Herve was anxious to get the ball rolling and needed some fast traction, he was also prepared to wait for the right fit for his brand. Our strategy—picking A-list actresses to borrow his dresses for red carpet events—also significantly improved our chances of getting international press for Herve.

> *"You need to have the right celebrity for the right project for the right market for the right brand."*
> —FABIO MANCONE, GLOBAL DIRECTOR OF
> LICENSING AND COMMUNICATIONS FOR THE GIORGIO
> ARMANI GROUP, IN *WOMEN'S WEAR DAILY*

Jay Godfrey struggled to decide whether reality stars were the right girls for his brand. In an earlier chapter, I wrote about Jay and Eva Mendes. Superstar Eva was one of the first celebrities to wear one of Jay's flirty dresses, so his logical assumption was that more A-list actresses would follow. The price point of most of his dresses range from $300 to $400, in contrast to Hervé L. Leroux's dresses, which sell for thousands of dollars. Jay's keen business sense told him he needed to find his own strategy and celebrities. Eva opened retail doors for Jay's business, but once he landed numerous accounts, he understood more about his customers, who were watching the Kardashians and *The Hills* alumni. Reaching for the A-list actresses (for Jay's brand) continues but, at the same time, he opened the doors to B- and C-list actresses who still influence his demographic and sales, as mentioned in chapter 2.

Since we'd worked together while she was at A Pea in the Pod, Mona Liss—now working as PR director for IKEA—already knew about my philosophy of pairing the right celebrity with the right brand. Mona hired me to help her find the perfect celebrity host for an IKEA event. We tossed around many names, but found our perfect host in Amy Sedaris. Says Mona:

> For an IKEA event titled "Home Is the Most Important Place in the World," IKEA hired comedienne/actress/author Amy Sedaris as the celebrity host who kept the evening entertaining and fun. IKEA believes FUN is central to everyday living. At the time of the event, we showed a film to 350 editors about everyday people's homes—lifestyles of all ages and ethnic groups. Amy had just written a book, *I Like You: Hospitality Under the Influence*, and was the perfect fit with stories of her pet rabbit Dusty and running a cupcake-and-cheese-ball business out of her home kitchen!

Amy was amazing! She even had a custom Dutch-girl costume made for the event. Editors can be a jaded crowd of men and women, but Amy's twisted stories about her pet rabbit and wacky business in the heart of New York City put smiles on their faces and garnered a few big belly laughs, too. Mona wanted the IKEA event to be fun, and Amy delivered.

I'm glad Mona and I could bounce ideas off each other, but we had a history of respect, having already worked together. When Hasbro Games contacted me to help launch a DVD version of Trivial Pursuit, it already had specific ideas about finding the right celebrities. The company was hosting open-to-the-public media events in a few key cities. It had a script already written for the celebrity, so everything was planned right down to the minute. Since I had a budget to hire Hasbro's celebrity, I went right to my list of agents. The first question an agent will ask is, "What's your budget?" So I was pretty excited when a promising young actor's name was brought up. He is a huge star now, but at the time he was mostly known for his work in a popular network sitcom. It was clear that his star was on the rise, however. I believed he was perfect for this opportunity, but the decision makers at Hasbro weren't convinced. To complicate matters, the actor—in a scene right out of *Entourage*—requested that Hasbro hire a fellow actor from the show to accompany him. He was even willing to lower his fee slightly to make sure his friend got paid out of the deal.

In my experience, if one of the parties involved throws too many layers into the mix, a deal can quickly become sour. It's not rocket science; adding more people to the process slows down decisions and negotiations. I didn't have enough fight left after rounds and rounds of calls and e-mails, so I ended up acquiescing to the Hasbro decision makers and let the actor go. Hasbro ended up hiring Naomi Judd, Nancy Kerrigan, Joe Piscopo, and radio DJ Casey Kasem—none of whom have the broad appeal of the actor I wanted to hire.

It's also best to find celebrities who aren't already associated with multiple brands with conflicting images. *The New Yorker* recently did a feature story on the "Godfather of Punk," Iggy Pop. While it used to be a well-kept secret that stars received freebies, Pop proudly boasts that he wears Brioni, Dolce & Gabbana, Chrome Hearts, and Versace—free of charge. He said, "Now I'll wear a pair of whatever anyone gives me." All these brands are, in my opinion, good fits for Iggy's image, except for Brioni, which is a little more boardroom than the rocker's usual image. If you had a product that was more on the high-end or luxury side, you'd probably want to steer clear of someone whose main influence is with the rock and roll crowd, even if he's been associated with similar brands in the past.

THE PERFECT PARTNER

In addition to collaborating with the right celebrities, companies can find success by partnering up with another business that has similar sensibilities. One of my clients, Me & Ro, combined its talents with those of another client of mine, Alber Elbaz of Lanvin, in the early 2000s. The world-class designer ended up being a launch pad for the jewelry company. One of Me & Ro's founders, Michelle Quan (an ex-model) had modeled for Alber in the early days of her career, and Alber knew of her brand's inspirational nature. So, when he had a vision of modern matte gold-hammered earrings, bangle bracelets, and rings for his first show for Lanvin, but had no experience in the jewelry-making business, he knew whom to call. The pair created a special edition collection to complement Alber's show and bring international attention to Me & Ro. With Lanvin's booming global clientele, Me & Ro benefited from exclusive sales in its New York and Miami stores.

Swarovski's partnerships also help to keep the brand in front of demographics that might be considered unusual for crystal. In 2004, Swarovski created a gigantic star that tops the Rockefeller Center Christmas tree in New York City. This relationship has lasted since then. And because Swarovski operates a store in Rockefeller Center that sells Christmas-oriented merchandise, the match is a perfect fit. Swarovski was also a sponsor for the most recent film version of *The Phantom of the Opera* and created the crystal chandelier that featured prominently in the movie. Pushing that partnership even further, I helped to arrange for a version of that chandelier to be displayed at the Fashion Institute of Design & Merchandising's annual Art of Motion Picture Costume Design exhibit, which showcases samples of Academy Award–nominated costumes.

THE BATTLE *for* ZIYI

In the early 2000s, many huge fashion brands were just opening retail stores in China, so that market and clientele was an important expansion for them. Chinese actress Ziyi Zhang was attending the Academy Awards as part of the cast of *Crouching Tiger, Hidden Dragon*, which was nominated for several awards that year. She did not speak English at the time, but her manager in China answered my inquiries in perfect English. He was honest with me and said she really only knew the big fashion brand names that were already in China. I didn't bother sending photographs of gowns from lesser-known clients because he wouldn't be interested. Luckily, Escada had a store in China, so when I said that Escada would love to dress Ziyi Zhang for the Oscars, she was very interested in seeing what it had to offer.

She was filming a movie in Las Vegas, but was able to take a side trip to Los Angeles where I met with her, her mother, and her manager. She tried on a bunch of gowns, including a really beautiful floral sequined cheongsam-style gown with a high collar. Her mother felt she should wear something traditional for her first time at the Oscars as a Chinese actress, and this dress was it. There were a few things on the dress that had to be tweaked, so I sent it to Germany for the alterations. Ziyi wasn't coming back to Los Angeles until the night before the Oscars. I crossed my fingers that everything would be perfect when I presented her with the finished gown.

I put it at the back of my mind until I got a call from a not-so-friendly competitor of mine who owned another agency. She is known for her brash, in-your-face manner, which appeals to some clients, whereas I am more subtly persistent. We each had our own clients and rarely ran into each other—until the Ziyi Zhang situation, that is. "I hear we're going to be working together," she said when she called. At first I didn't know what she was talking about, but it turned out she represented shoe company Jimmy Choo at the time.

"I'm doing the shoes for Ziyi Zhang's dress," she said.

This was the first time I had heard that. Escada did its own shoes and handbags. "Of course Ziyi can make her own decision, but I know Escada's making shoes to go with her gown, too," I replied.

Days later, I was visiting one of the Oscar gifting suites at the L'Ermitage hotel in Beverly Hills. I represented Swarovski, and it had one of the biggest suites, with displays of crystal chandeliers, crystal handbags, and crystal jewelry. It was really quite amazing. I was in the suite talking with Nadja Swarovski when a bigwig at Jimmy Choo marched in with my competitor, who wore a sly grin on her face.

"Where is this Susan Ashbrook?" the bigwig barked at Nadja. "I want to talk to this Susan Ashbrook."

I was standing right there, so I said, "I'm Susan Ashbrook." I knew who Ms. Bigwig was, but I didn't know what she looked like, so at the time I had no idea who this crazy woman was.

"Nadja should fire you right now for what you're doing to me. What do you think you're doing stopping Ziyi Zhang from wearing my shoes? Don't you know how important it is to have a Chinese woman wearing my brand?" she asked.

I was dumbfounded. I think my mouth was actually hanging open. I couldn't believe that this woman was attacking me in front of a room full of people. And she was trying to get a client to fire me. This was probably the one time in my career when I almost cried. She was just that abrasive.

"Escada is my client," I replied, struggling to keep it together, "and my job is to represent the brand in the best way I know how. It's up to Ziyi to make her own decision."

Ms. Bigwig flipped her hair and walked out, but not before saying, "I'll make sure you never work in this town again!"

The day before the Oscars, I got a call from Ziyi's manager saying that Ziyi's flight was arriving very late and that she wasn't going to get to her hotel in Beverly Hills until 2:00 a.m.

"Okay, I'll meet her at two in the morning with my seamstress," I said. While I was waiting in the lobby with my seamstress, in walks my competitor with the goddamned Jimmy Choo shoes. I'm thinking, you have got to be kidding me—at two o'clock in the morning I have to face this? There we both were, each vying for an actress who we thought embodied exactly what our clients' brands needed to be as they expanded to China.

At last we got called up to the room and Ziyi tried on the dress. It fit perfectly. Then it was time for her to choose the shoes.

In addition to the personally delivered Escada shoes and personally delivered Jimmy Choo shoes, Stuart Weitzman had sent some shoes without a personal escort. Of course, these are the shoes Ziyi ended up wearing. In this case, neither my competitor nor I got the celeb we wanted, but we had good reason to go after her: We had a sound strategic reason why her image fit the direction in which our client companies were moving.

Knowing a client's demographics and customers are important to me, and this information is integral in my search for the right stars to be associated with its products. Once I've figured it out, my persistence to put product on these celebrities kicks into high gear. That day, with my competitor, I thought about throwing it all away in a moment of exasperation, but the fact remains: Finding a celebrity marketing partner with the perfect image for your brand is difficult, but essential to success.

Learning the Landscape

- Know your demographic. If your merchandise appeals to twenty-year-olds, Julia Roberts and George Clooney won't even be a blip on their radar.

- It's okay to be strategic and handpick celebrities who you'd like to see with your product, but be prepared for it to take some time. However, if you see your merchandise blowing up in the media, blast it to anyone and everyone who has a screen presence.

- If you have a niche product, consider stars who will appeal to that specific demographic: Latino celebrities, celebrities who cook, celebrities who own dogs, reality stars, morning news journalists, etc.

- Celebrities are born every day. If your dream celebrity who's *just* right for your product doesn't bite even after continued persistence, move on.

CHAPTER 11

BUILDING
RELATIONSHIPS

Ralph Waldo Emerson penned the famous words "Hitch your wagon to a star" about 150 years ago, and I like to apply that saying to my work in hitching products to the stars of Hollywood. I built my business on this idea, and I know that the most important component, the glue that keeps the product and celebrity hitched together, are the personal relationships between all parties involved.

Relationships are vital to building any business, and celebrity marketing is no different. When I first started Film Fashion, I hand-delivered clothing samples and tried to meet everyone in person. We all like to work with people we know and trust. Every celebrity who walked through my door knew I wouldn't call the people at *The National Enquirer* to offer up any confidences (although I did call them to let them know about a client's product on a celebrity).

You might think I was on friendly terms with the seven thousand celebrities in my database. Truthfully, it wasn't the celebrities themselves I became friendly with; more than likely I was friendly with their support staff. These are all the people I mentioned in chapter 9: the publicist, manager, stylist, agent, costume designer, and sometimes the best friend, parent, or husband.

> *"Having a strong and lasting relationship with one particular celebrity can certainly lead to new relationships with future celebrities; after all, celebrities have other girlfriends who may also be celebrities, so building a relationship with them is really no different than how you may approach building a relationship with the girl next door, who, if she likes your service, may recommend you to her best friend, too. Also, you should consider that one celebrity might lead to another through the relationship you cultivate with their agent or manager. I am never opposed to offering to dress an agent or manager of a major celebrity; again, it is all about building your network and creating enduring relationships."* —ELIZABETH MASON, OWNER OF VINTAGE COUTURE SHOP THE PAPER BAG PRINCESS

For the first three years of my business, I worked from my living room, serving up couture finery to my clients. I learned quickly that my new business was about servicing celebrities whenever I got a call at odd times and weekends. They knew I worked from home, had quick access to designers, and could provide fashion-forward goods for a last-minute appearance. I wasn't building personal friendships with celebrities, but I was building business relationships for the future.

More important than a friendship with the celebrity him- or herself were the relationships I developed with celebrity stylists and publicists. Those relationships don't guarantee the stars will walk the carpet in a client's creation, but they do guarantee an honest response and a chance that a designer's garment will end up being seen by a celebrity.

If you get the opportunity to meet a celebrity, jump to do it; no one will represent your product better than you. I know plenty of people who get tongue-tied when they meet a celebrity, but I've always reminded myself to "keep it real." No matter how many famous faces I see or how much adrenaline races through my body, I try to be myself. It doesn't matter what business you're in; relationships are important, and you want to work with nice people, people who show up when they say they're going to, who deliver when they say they're going to—people you can count on. Celebrities and their inner circle will see you mean well and will want to work with you because of this.

> *"Networking is very important, whether you're a CEO or an entrepreneur. Nothing is linear anymore, and the connections you make—you never know what is going to come of them."* —MINDY GROSSMAN,
> **CEO OF THE HOME SHOPPING NETWORK**

Fashion designer Catherine Malandrino sent a personal note to Mary J. Blige a few years ago to let her know she was a fan and to invite the pop star to her birthday celebration. She never expected Mary J. to show up, but she did, and their friendship has continued for years. Mary J. even helped Catherine open her store in Los Angeles when Catherine needed some star power to get media to write about the store. Let's face it, if you and I wrote a note to Mary J. Blige inviting her to our birthday celebration, chances are slim she would attend. However, there are a handful of local VIPs who might attend an event or party we threw, so why not start there? If it's an election year, a politician would probably welcome the chance to mingle with neighborhood voters, and you might start a relationship with a future mayor. You might even consider inviting a few local journalists as guests. It's important to think about the big picture, as a relationship can grow over time.

Photo by PR Photos

Designer Catherine Malandrino
with her pal Mary J. Blige.

BUILDING RELATIONSHIPS
from the HEART

Relationships take time to build, but one way to build strong relationships with celebrities is to find out whether they have a passion for a charity or are involved in philanthropic work. If the celebrities you are courting are concerned about protecting the environment or curing cancer, make a donation to their charity. Or, become a sponsor of their charity; it increases the chances that you'll find yourself at the same gala ball or fundraiser. (It's also, of course, helpful if you share a sincere passion for the cause with the celebrity.) Backing the same charity often gets you access to celebrities, and will certainly build goodwill and rapport. This endeavor can get expensive, but you could always make a smaller investment, like donating product to an auction that benefits the celebrity's charity of choice.

> *"Relationships are everything! You need to take care to grow and foster them. My relationships are the reason why stores open early, stay open late, loan me never-before-borrowed pieces, and make custom dresses in twenty-four hours."* —ANYA SARRE, HEAD FASHION STYLIST, *ENTERTAINMENT TONIGHT* AND *THE INSIDER*

Jessica Alba, for example, helped a shoe client (at no cost) to promote "the Jessica" high heel. A percentage of sales of the shoe benefited Keep a Child Alive, a charity she supports. The small shoe company, Rickard Shah, had been providing Jessica shoes to wear to red carpet events, and Jessica just loved their shoes. She has her choice of any shoe brand to borrow from—Christian Louboutin, Manolo Blahnik, Jimmy Choo—but she preferred working with this little company, and it was getting a lot of press from the connection. Rickard Shah would make her custom colors and a five-inch heel instead of a four-inch one—it was a very nice, organic relationship.

Film Fashion had the idea to name her favorite shoe "the Jessica," make it in lots of colors, and call the line "the Icon Collection." We planned an event at a store in Los Angeles that carried the shoes and asked her to host it. It was a long shot—would a celebrity host a shoe event? But she said yes, mainly because Rickard Shah said it would donate a percentage of the sales to Jessica's favorite charity. It was a great collaboration and a creative way to get the celebrity involved—and do some good, too.

I mentioned my work with Heart Truth in chapter 6; I used my involvement with that campaign to network for Film Fashion and build relationships for my other clients. Talk about the pyramid theory! By 2009, I had five fashion clients involved in Heart Truth and dressed celebrity models Amanda Bynes, Susan Lucci, Daisy Fuentes, Jane Kaczmarek, and Samantha Harris. The campaign's Red Dress fashion show continues to

Photo by PR Photos

Find a charity close to your heart as a means of building a relationship with a star. Jane Seymour's Open Hearts Foundation is about keeping an open heart to face life's challenges.

promote healthy women, but at the same time put Film Fashion's designer clients in front of worldwide media.

If you decide to find a charity close to your heart as a means of building a relationship with a star, two other key elements are consistency and patience. Don't expect to make connections right out of the gate. The best part of working with a charity is your sincere desire to help. From there, you can network to figure out the best way to present your product and incorporate it into the mix.

Let's say you are an animal lover and have decided to find a charity devoted to helping animals. (I picked this example because it's my favorite type of charity!) One of the best websites to use to find that perfect animal rights group and the celebrities associated with it is www.LookToTheStars. org. There, and elsewhere on the Web, you'll find many animal charities to consider, including PETA, the Humane Society, Farm Sanctuary, Greenpeace, Oceana, Best Friends Animal Society, World Wildlife Fund, and Wildlife Warriors Worldwide.

> *"One of the greatest attributes associated with the celebrities we cover is how they have used their notoriety and their popularity to become advocates for others."* — VICTORIA LASDON ROSE, PUBLISHER OF *US WEEKLY*, IN THE MAGAZINE'S OCTOBER 2010 "STARS WHO CARE" ISSUE

Pierce Brosnan's charitable concerns are many, including working with the environmental advocacy group the Natural Resources Defense Council in its efforts to stop the Navy deployment of sonar systems that have been shown to kill whales, dolphins, seals, and other marine mammals. He is also a member of Oceana, and profits from his paintings are distributed to the charities he supports.

Best Friends Animal Society works with the public and with humane groups all across the country to realize a vision of a world with no homeless pets. The celebrities who have come out for this charity include Adrian Grenier, Charlize Theron, Clint Eastwood, Jessica Biel, and Willie Nelson, to name just a few.

Blake Mycoskie, who founded Toms Shoes in 2006, gives away one pair of shoes to a child in need in a developing country for each pair of his shoes purchased. In 2010, the company delivered its millionth pair of shoes to a child in Argentina. Mycoskie has collaborated with celebrities like Charlize Theron and the Olsen Twins, and with other organizations. He says, "It feels good, but it's also good for business, for building morale, which is equally important."

Photo by Kerry Perez

Bo Derek models the Swarovski denim jacket she designed for an auction that raised both money for a charity initiative and brand awareness.

Swarovski has a huge marketing budget and a team of PR experts all over the world to bring awareness to the brand and its initiatives, but the crystal maker has continued its partnership with SOS Children's Villages since 1949. In 2007, Swarovski partnered with the U.S. arm of the charity to create a celebrity denim jacket auction on eBay.

Since I was Swarovski's celebrity expert, the job of asking celebrities to help draw attention to the charity fell on my shoulders. I contacted many celebrities and asked them to design a jean jacket to support World Orphan Week. Many of them were eager to come together for a bigger cause (and we got lots of press for the crystal jackets). The celebrities we got on board included Finola Hughes, Jessica Alba, Laila Ali, Eric Dane, Rebecca Gayheart, Angie Harmon, Reba McEntire, Katharine McPhee, Sara Ramirez, Carrie Underwood, Vanessa Williams, and Jordin Sparks.

Many of the celebrities expressed their excitement about the project, including Jordin, who, according to SOS-USA.org, said:

> A relative of mine works for SOS Children's Village in Florida, so when she asked if I'd be interested in supporting the children by designing a jacket with Swarovski crystals, I said yes! I decided I wanted to have the jacket's design reflect something about who I am, so first I used geometric patterns that remind me of my home state of Arizona and the American Indian culture there. If you look closely, you'll see the letter *S* in the pattern. That stands for Sparks. And you'll also see little hearts placed here and there. Throughout my run on *American Idol*, I made a heart sign with my fingers over my heart to let my fans and family know how much I love them.

IN *the* PINK

It can also be helpful to befriend the leaders of charities as you look to develop synergy between your product and a celebrity. Chicagoan Nancy Avner is just the type of person you'd want to connect with. She grew up with a great-grandmother, a grandmother, and a mother who were all diagnosed with breast and ovarian cancer. As a teenager, Nancy got half of the students at her high school to walk and raise funds for Susan G. Komen for the Cure, which supports breast cancer research. Nancy's compassion kicked into high gear when she learned at twenty-two that she had the same mutated gene, which meant she had an 87 percent chance of getting ovarian cancer. The news altered the course of her life. Nancy founded Bright Pink (BeBrightPink.org), a national nonprofit organization that provides education and support to young women who are at high risk for breast and ovarian cancer. She organized yoga parties and cooking classes to network with women looking for support and information about breast and ovarian cancer. The charity grew so much that Nancy left her full-time job. Wrigley stepped up to donate up to $75,000, derived from sales of Orbit White gum marked with the Bright Pink logo.

Long before October—Breast Cancer Awareness Month—rolls around, I'd suggest meeting up with Nancy—and there are dedicated "Nancys" in whatever part of the world you reside. Let's say you are angling for a red carpet moment to bring awareness to your Main Street store. If your store can align with a worthwhile charity, why not offer clever tie-ins? To stick with the breast cancer charity example, you could offer up pink yoga mats, pink cooking pans, pink hair ornaments, pink bangles, and pink champagne to kick off the month. Your next step is to look for celebrities or VIPs who have been touched by breast cancer, either personally or through their immediate family. Once you confirm a VIP—or better yet, a few VIPs—then you have a good shot at some serious press attention.

A VIP influencer in your city might not be a movie star; it could be the local weather person. She could model something pink each day from your store to publicize the charity event. Whether it's breast cancer or heart awareness or animal rights, charities can be the partnership you need to match up clients with a worthy cause.

Find three that touch your heart and call them today. See if there is a way to work together. If you deliver the VIP, set up the location for their next event, or donate product or a portion of product sales, you might have found the gateway to giving back while still keeping the focus on marketing your store. I promise a celebrity will consider your idea if it's a way to raise awareness for a charity close to his or her heart.

Nancy Gale, designer and owner of Jamah Handbags, designed her own charity to help promote her product. She describes it as a *"Project Runway* meets *The Apprentice* and reality meets substance . . ."

> Recognizing the importance of giving back, I was inspired to make a difference and created In True Fashion, an apprenticeship program founded on cause, commerce, and consciousness. In a sentence, In True Fashion builds self-esteem and work ethic in American youth through hands-on participation and promotes the value of products that are made in the USA. The students in the program participate in the manufacturing process at Jamah, from product inception, to financing, to marketing, and their hard work culminates in finished bags that are exposed to the world. They also get a chance to design their own bags, and the designs are voted on. The winning bag is taken into production and sold to the public as a new addition to the Jamah Collection. Every time the winning bag is purchased, a portion of its proceeds goes to our partner, Network for Teaching Entrepreneurship, a nonprofit organization, and the student's high school.

The next step for Nancy and her charity is partnering with a celebrity to help get her message out. Nancy is following my guidelines by creating a realistic target list and examining the relationships she already has in place. Ashton Kutcher, with his incredible Twitter influence, might be a good place to start!

THE NICHE CONNECTION

Finding your own niche can also open doors for you and align your goals with a celebrity's. Gustavo Cadile, a fashion designer and immigrant from

Argentina's own Gustavo Cadile.

Argentina, knew that being Latin was an advantage he had over other designers. To help build awareness for his brand, he started doing his own celebrity marketing by targeting Latino stars. He quickly landed Eva Longoria, Daisy Fuentes, and Thalia. These Latin ladies wanted to help a fellow Latino and were eager to wear his beautiful dresses to help him.

Gustavo started out in Florida working in a Neiman Marcus stockroom. He studied the gowns and dresses of all the great fashion designers on his lunch break, and one head saleswoman in the department couldn't help but notice his steady presence. She finally asked the young man why he was working in the stockroom if fashion design was really his passion, giving him the confidence he needed to push on. When he eventually began designing on his own, playing up his Latin background was the tool he used to build relationships with the stars who would really put him on the map.

Photo by PR Photos

Designer Gustavo Cadile found a niche by targeting
Latina stars like Eva Longoria to wear his dresses.

If you're thinking you're a little guy who can't compete with the big guys of fashion, think of Gustavo's story. Gustavo attacked that Latin niche with gusto and glee. He had enough confidence in himself to send photos of his dresses to the movie stars he wanted, plunging into the world of celebrity marketing with the Latino women he believed would embrace his designs.

MAKING *a* DEAL

While many brands are able to build strong relationships with celebrities through personal friendships, similar charitable concerns, or shared values or backgrounds, it's good to keep in mind that some relationships in Hollywood aren't organic and are in fact downright costly. These are the outright sponsorship or endorsements deals that we've discussed throughout the book. Says Merle Ginsberg:

> Look at Julia Roberts, Cate Blanchett, and George Clooney with Armani. That took years. It takes a lot of money to create these relationships. Overseas trips, favors, product, work, effort, and schmoozing and payback.

I represented a number of luxury jewelry brands that grew tired of bringing jewelry worth the cost of a house to stylists' homes before big events, only to learn the jewelry didn't make the cut. Chopard instead enlisted ambassadors Charlize Theron, Penelope Cruz, and Marion Cotillard to wear its jewelry to the Academy Awards (and it's rumored that they were paid). Chopard, along with other jewelry houses with hefty marketing budgets, found it cheaper to "buy" a celebrity, resulting in international media coverage. Hopefully you can find a more affordable path to getting your product seen with a star, but it's good to know how the guys with the big budgets do things, too.

Learning the Landscape

- Remember that relationships take time to build, so start slow and steady.

- If the opportunity exists to connect in person—do it! Everyone likes to work with someone they know personally, respect, and can count on.

- Support staff are the stepping-stones to decision makers. Don't discount working with assistants, because your kindness and good manners might just be your ace card to getting in front of a celebrity.

- Write personal notes. Your small business can stand out over corporate coolness due to your individual touch.

- Celebrities have a passion for giving. Pick a charity that means something to you and you'll find celebrities that share it.

- What makes your business different? Embrace a niche or specialty so you stand out as you build relationships with celebs.

CONCLUSION

When I started Film Fashion and began doing celebrity marketing for the red carpet, I used to think to myself, *Well, this can't last forever. People will grow tired of celebrities.* But that hasn't happened at all. In fact, looking back, it seems like a very strange thing to have thought. Celebrities today hold just as much influence as they did when I started out. Fashion is always evolving, and the same can be said about the world of celebrities. Just when the public consciousness has become saturated with a celebrity, in walks another, ready to take over the spotlight with his or her own sense of style. The trick is to learn the challenges of celebrity marketing to help propel your dreams—and your merchandise. Keep your product eye-catching, relevant, and desired with a goal for longevity by changing up your celebrity endorsers along with the times. You'll find that your brand will continue to stay on top as long as you continue to get the word out.

Now is an exciting time to begin your celebrity-marketing adventure. We now have more means of communicating with key players and consumers themselves than I could have imagined when I founded Film Fashion. If you can adapt to this ever-changing landscape, stay true to your brand, and expand how you communicate to your consumer (especially through social media), you're poised for a great deal of success. As you think about celebrity marketing, do your homework. Start building your brand. Let people know about your company. Expand your boundaries by finding creative partners. All this is just the tip of the iceberg toward taking your business further than you've ever imagined.

At the end of the day, when you differentiate your brand to stand above and apart from others, you are on your way to a successful brand campaign. What I hope to have shown you in this book is a simple truth: Celebrities will get you there faster.

ABOUT *the* AUTHOR

Susan Ashbrook has been involved in celebrity product placement for twenty years. She founded and pioneered Film Fashion, the first fashion product placement company in Los Angeles. Her first client was Ralph Lauren, and she went on to match top celebrities with a roster of clients that included Lanvin, Chopard, Swarovski, Escada, Isaac Mizrahi, and many more. She has also consulted for non-fashion brands like Nikon, Hasbro Games, and MasterCard. Ashbrook sold Film Fashion to the PR powerhouse Rogers & Cowan in 2008.